W9-BLU-301

BEYOND
log cabin

Kerry Gadd

Martingale
& COMPANY

Bothell, Washington

EDITORIAL
MANAGING EDITOR
Judy Poulos
EDITORIAL ASSISTANT
Ella Martin
JUNIOR PRODUCTION EDITOR
Heather Straton

PHOTOGRAPHY
Andy Payne, Richard Weinstein
STYLING
Kathy Tripp

PRODUCTION AND DESIGN
PRODUCTION DIRECTOR
Anna Maguire
PRODUCTION COORDINATOR
Meredith Johnston
DESIGN MANAGER
Drew Buckmaster
ASSISTANT DESIGNER AND COVER DESIGN
Sheridan Packer

PUBLISHED BY Martingale & Company
PO Box 118
Bothell, WA 98041-0118
USA
www.patchwork.com
Library of Congress Cataloging-in-Publishing Data Available

FORMATTED BY J.B. Fairfax Press

PRINTED BY Toppan Printing Co. Hong Kong
04 03 02 01 00 99   654321
© LibertyOne Limited 1999

BEYOND LOG CABIN
ISBN 1 56477 284 5

Martingale
& COMPANY

That Patchwork Place is an imprint of
Martingale & Company.

MISSION STATEMENT
We are dedicated to providing quality products and service by working together to inspire creativity and to enrich the lives we touch.

Contents

Introduction

When I was a child, I was always creating things with my hands. Every Sunday, my mother would rake under my bed to remove the week's projects. I was very messy then, and I haven't changed much to this day – I call it creative chaos!

Both my mother and grandmother made clothing for the family, so I was introduced to sewing at a fairly early age. I learned to sew by making Barbie dolls' clothes by hand, as I wasn't allowed near the sewing machine.

I first became interested in quilting about fourteen years ago, when I saw a photograph of a quilt in a magazine. Following the instructions carefully, I constructed the ugliest quilt ever seen. It finished up in the dog's kennel! After taking a patchwork class to learn the basics, I went on to make traditional quilts. Quickly realizing that I would never have the time to make all the quilts I wanted to, I began to make miniatures and small quilts. I tried both rotary cutting and foundation-piecing techniques and found both of them equally satisfying.

A workshop with Margaret Miller introduced me to methods of changing basic block divisions. From this, I realized that not only could the divisions within a block be altered, but the whole quilt grid itself could also be changed. Creating a distorted grid produced some startling results. Traditional blocks took on a whole new slant and, when combined, they created wonderful secondary designs.

I have had an ongoing love affair with Log Cabin quilts for a long time. Over the last seven years I have developed a method of making quilts based on distorted grids, in combination with the traditional Log Cabin block. Using foundation piecing for the construction process and the traditional Log Cabin design for the units formed by the distorted grid gives a totally different appearance to the traditional Log Cabin design. Every time I make one of these quilts, I can see another design emerging and immediately put it into my design folder for future reference. The possibilities are endless. I do not limit myself to the traditional spiraling Log Cabin block, but also experiment with different variations.

In this book, I want to give quiltmakers a new way to achieve a different look for the time-honoured Log Cabin quilt. The techniques involved are not speedy, but they are very accurate and the results can be unexpected. No matter how carefully you plan a quilt, at some stage the quilt 'takes over' and the result is often quite different from what you expected or planned.

Although the process I use is quite complex, even beginners can, with care, construct the projects. Understanding basic patchwork skills is essential, both for drafting and quilt construction techniques.

Hopefully, this book will take Log Cabin quilts one step further and open up a whole new area for experimentation. I hope, too, that after making some of the projects in this book, quiltmakers will begin to develop their own designs.

I have tried to include all the information necessary to construct the quilts. Please read these early chapters thoroughly before beginning to make a quilt, as you will be continually referred back to them. Finally, I strongly advise you to do the drafting exercise on page 8, before attempting any of the projects. This will make the instructions a lot easier to understand.

Have fun and enjoy.

About the Author

For the last nine years, I have been teaching quiltmaking to both beginners and advanced students. The classes are all based on miniature quiltmaking and foundation piecing, and I also offer design workshops based on block manipulation and drafting. I really enjoy teaching, as it was my profession before marriage and raising my family.

Over the last couple of years I have contributed projects to the *Australian Patchwork & Quilting* magazine and have had work published in *Quilter's Newsletter* magazine, *Textile Fibre Forum, Down Under Quilts* and the Quilters' Guild magazine, *The Template.* I have had work exhibited throughout Australia, Asia, Japan, New Zealand, Germany and America.

Drafting the Units

Traditional

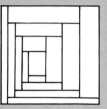

Even logs

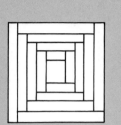

Wide-narrow

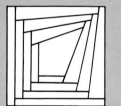

Even-uneven, version 1

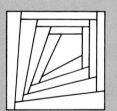

Even-uneven, version 2

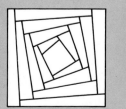

All uneven

These quilts are made by a method which produces exceptional accuracy. This is not a fast technique. It is a slow and fairly complex process, and involves a wide range of patchwork techniques from drafting to piecing. The projects begin with simple designs and graduate through to quite complex ones. Before you begin, read this section carefully.

LOG CABIN BLOCKS AND VARIATIONS

The basic Log Cabin block consists of strips of fabric, called logs, pieced around a central shape. In the traditional block, the logs are pieced, beginning in the center and spiraling around it in a clockwise or counter-clockwise direction. The Courthouse Steps block is pieced by adding the logs to opposite sides of the center, working from side to side.

Because the quilt projects presented in this book are all based on distorted grids, the resulting units are oddly shaped. All the variations possible for the Log Cabin block can still be applied, with the obvious difference that the resulting center shapes are not always square.

There are lots of ways to change the appearance of the traditional Log Cabin block, such as different log widths, uneven logs, crazy logs, varying the order of the piecing, or changing the shape of the center. The variations that appear in the projects are shown here, and both the traditional block and the distorted variations are shown.

■ **Even logs** All the logs are the same width with an equal number on either side of the center.

■ **Wide-narrow** There are four narrow and three wide logs on either side of the center shape. The center shape of the unit is now off-center.

■ **Even-uneven, version 1** There are four even logs and three uneven logs on either side of the center. The longest outside logs are even.

■ **Even-uneven, version 2** There are four uneven logs and three even logs on either side of the center. The longest outside logs are uneven.

■ **All uneven** There is an equal number of logs on either side of the center shape.

The quilt projects in this book are pieced using this range of variations and combinations of them. Pay careful attention to the layout plans, and follow the drafting directions and diagrams closely.

The logs are drafted onto the units in a particular order to make the designs work. In the instructions for the projects, the drafting order is indicated by a symbol •→

THE GRID

Nearly all traditional patchwork blocks are drafted onto a grid. Traditionally, these grids, with the exception of the eight-pointed star, are all even. That is, a square is divided into equal divisions across and down, and the block is drafted onto this.

Blocks, when they are put together, form another kind of grid – a quilt grid, which may have straight sets, diagonal sets, be with or without sashing strips, alternate blocks, etc. This is the quilt surface.

In the system I use, the grid I refer to is a quilt grid, not a block grid.

All of my quilts are developed on grids that are either symmetrical or asymmetrical. They are nearly always diagonal settings with no sashing strips separating the units.

The quilt grid is developed first. This is done by marking specific increments, using dots across and down, on a sheet of graph paper. The units that form within the grid are then developed by drawing diagonal lines in both directions within the grid divisions. It is a simple exercise of joining dot to dot diagonally, in both directions, on the graph paper. This results in oddly shaped units that are set on-point.

Each unit has a Log Cabin variation drafted onto it. Because you are working with a distorted grid, nearly every unit must be drafted separately to obtain a master pattern for tracing onto the foundation. If the grid is symmetrical, you may be lucky enough to have some units which repeat.

Every unit within the grid must have an identifying number so you know where it belongs – like a road map. The grid also helps you keep track of what units you have marked and their placement within the quilt.

Each project in the book has a quilt layout plan, showing the grid it was designed on, with the identifying numbers for the units and the directions for drafting the logs.

Figure 1 shows the grid for 'The Hot Line' on page 36, with all the units identified and log drafting directions shown. The symbol (•→) indicates that you begin at the dot and mark in the direction of the arrow.

IMPERIAL V. METRIC MEASUREMENTS

All measurements are given in both imperial and metric measurements. They are not conversions. Use one system or the other – don't try to combine them – they are not compatible. This is a recipe for disaster.

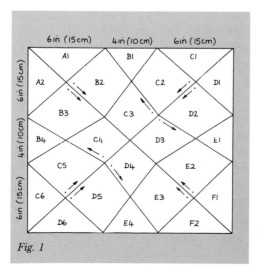

Fig. 1

Don't alter a given measurement if you think it's not correct. The measurements are for 'best fit'. Quilts made using imperial measurements will be slightly bigger than those made using metric measurements.

DRAFTING THE UNITS TO FULL SIZE

You will have to enlarge to full size, in sections, the scaled quilt plan for each project, to get it ready for drafting the logs and for marking the foundations.

Units within a quilt plan can be repeated, reversals of other units, or all different. I recommend that you draft every unit. This way, you know that they are all correct and that you haven't accidentally reversed the wrong unit. Each quilt has repeating corner and edge triangles. These are indicated with the instructions for each project.

A note about imperial and metric graph paper – all quilt unit groups in this book will fit into an area 11 in x 16 in (28 cm x 40 cm). If your graph paper is smaller than this, you will have to join sheets.

When drafting the grid to full size, only work with two divisions across and two divisions down at any one time. This results in four full units, and side and corner triangle units where applicable.

It is a good idea to indicate at the top of the graph paper the divisions you are marking and identify the resulting units. If you need to refer back to it, it can be found quickly. Also, label each sheet of graph paper you use, with the name of the quilt at the bottom.

I will use the grid from the quilt 'The Hot Line' on page 36 to demonstrate the process. Figure 2 is labeled with the units being drafted and the name of the quilt. It is also marked:

6 in (15 cm)
6 in (15 cm) + 4 in (10 cm)
4 in (10 cm)

This means that the divisions across the top of the planned grid are at 6 in + 4 in (15 cm + 10 cm) intervals and the divisions down the side are at 6 in + 4 in (15 cm + 10 cm) intervals.

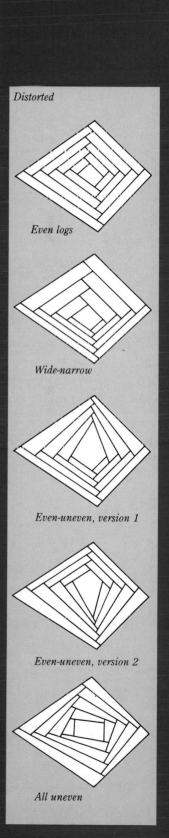

Distorted

Even logs

Wide-narrow

Even-uneven, version 1

Even-uneven, version 2

All uneven

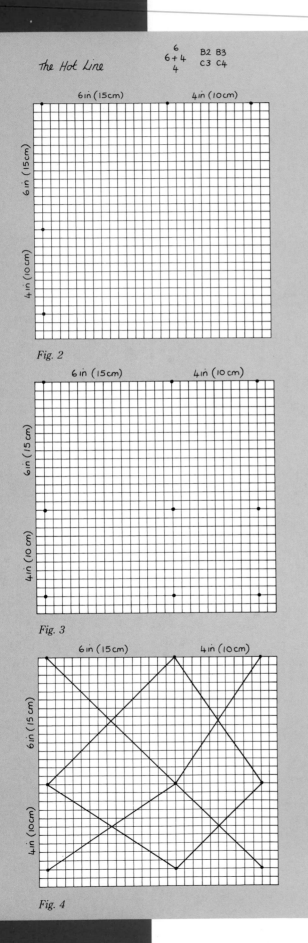

The Hot Line

6
6 + 4   B2   B3
4   C3   C4

6 in (15cm)   4 in (10 cm)

6 in (15 cm)

4 in (10 cm)

Fig. 2

6 in (15cm)   4 in (10 cm)

6 in (15 cm)

4 in (10 cm)

Fig. 3

6 in (15cm)   4 in (10 cm)

6 in (15 cm)

4 in (10cm)

Fig. 4

EXERCISE

I urge you to do this exercise before trying any of the projects.

1   Photocopy the grid or Quilt Layout Plan for 'The Hot Line' on page 7.

2   Place a sheet of cardboard on your work table. Place one sheet of graph paper on the cardboard.

3   Mark a dot at the top left-hand corner. The first division is at 6 in (15 cm), so measure across 6 in (15 cm) from the corner dot and make a dot. The next division is at 4 in (10 cm). Measure across 4 in (10 cm) from the previous dot and make another dot. The total distance across the top is 10 in (25 cm).

4   Repeat the last step down the left-hand side of the page. Note that you have already marked the corner dot. The total distance down is 10 in (25 cm) (Fig. 2).

5   Working from left to right across the paper and beginning at the 6 in (15 cm) mark, that is the second dot down on the left-hand side, mark a dot at 6 in (15 cm) and then at 4 in (10 cm). Slide the ruler down to the 4 in (10 cm) mark and again make dots at 6 in (15 cm) and 4 in (10 cm) intervals. You should have nine dots marked on the graph paper (Fig. 3).

6   Join the dots, diagonally, to form the grid (Fig. 4). Be as accurate as you can. If you make a mistake here, it will affect all the units. Check and double check that your initial increments are correct. I had to remake twenty units in 'Adrift' on page 72 because I didn't add correctly! So always double check.

7   You will now have a full-sized outline for the following units: B2, B3, C3, and C4. You will also have the corner triangles A1 and A2, and the edge triangles B1 and B4. If you draw a line across the top and down the left-hand side of the drafting, you will see the edge triangles form. Mark each unit roughly in the center, with its identifying number. Write 'top' at the top of the paper and 'left-hand side' down the left side. This allows you to find the corner and edge triangles easily when you need to (Fig. 5).

8   The next divisions to draft are at 4 in + 6 in (10 cm + 15 cm) across and 6 in + 4 in (15 cm + 10 cm) down. On another sheet of graph paper, draw the grid as before. This will repeat unit C3 and edge triangle B1 but will also give the following units: C2, D2, D3, corner triangles C1, D1 and edge triangle E1. Label each one in the center. Draw a line across the top and down the right-hand side through the dots. Label the graph paper with 'top' and 'right-hand side' (Fig. 6). You will now have all the units, corner and edge triangles drafted for the top of the quilt and you have identified the top and sides. Mark the name of the quilt at the bottom.

9 To draft the remaining units, corner and edge triangles, mark divisions at 6 in + 4 in (15 cm + 10 cm) across and 4 in + 6 in (10 cm + 15 cm) down. Draw the grid as before. The resulting units are C4, C5, D4, and D5; the corners are C6, D6, and the edge triangles are E4 and B4. Label all the units and triangles. Draw a line across the bottom and up the left-hand side. Write 'bottom' at the bottom of the paper and 'left-hand side' down the left side.

10 Mark the divisions at 4 in + 6 in (10 cm + 15 cm) across and 4 in + 6 in (10 cm + 15 cm) down. Draw the grid. The resulting units are D3, D4, E2, and E3; the corners F1, F2, and the edge triangles E1 and E4. Label all the units and triangles. Draw a line across the bottom and up the right-hand side. Write 'bottom' at the bottom of the paper and 'right-hand side' down the right side.

All the inner units and edge triangle units for 'The Hot Line' are now drafted. The top, bottom and sides have been identified, and all the units and triangles have been numbered. Note that as you work your way across and down the grid, you are moving across and down one increment (division) each time. This is why it is so important to label everything and place measurements and unit numbers at the top of each page of graph paper.

When you duplicate a unit or an edge triangle, place an X through it so you know not to draft logs onto it.

If I wanted to draft units in the middle of a quilt plan, I would look at the quilt layout plan and see what divisions these units are formed from, then draw a grid using those divisions. If you have trouble locating the divisions, lightly draw the vertical and horizontal lines of the grid on the photocopied layout plan (Fig. 7). This will enable you to see exactly what the divisions are.

The most important thing to remember when drafting the units is to make sure that you label everything and double-check all measurements.

DRAWING THE DESIGN ONTO THE UNITS

You are now ready to draft the Log Cabin variations onto the units. From this point onward, use the measurements on your ruler, not the graph paper.

When drafting the logs onto the units, draft the longest logs first (on the outside of the unit), and work in toward the center. (When you are piecing, you begin in the center with the shortest log and work toward the outside of the unit.)

To form a particular pattern, the logs must be positioned in a certain order for the design to work. On the layout plan I have indicated this by using a symbol (•→). The dot shows where to begin (the longest outside log) and the arrow

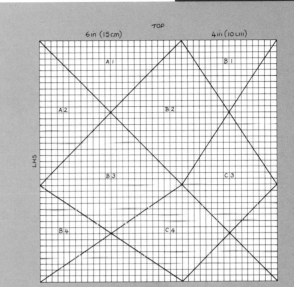

Fig. 5

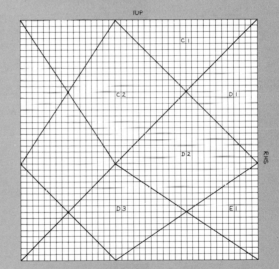

Fig. 6

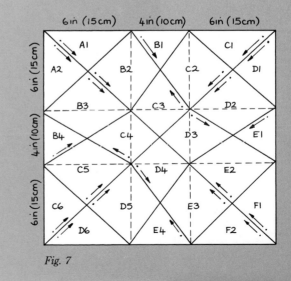

Fig. 7

shows the direction you work in when drafting the remainder of the logs, either clockwise or counter-clockwise. Always mark the symbol (•→) in the correct position on the drafted units before drafting the logs.

The log width can vary, as can the number of logs on either side of the center. If the unit has uneven logs, study the unit diagram for the project and pay particular attention to see whether the logs begin wide or narrow, or alternate.

Again, refer to the 'The Hot Line' layout plan on page 7 for the log placement and the direction of drafting. I will use units B2 and B3 and the edge triangle B1 to demonstrate. All the logs are 1 cm (³/8 in) wide.

Unit B2: Note the position of the dot and the arrow on the layout plan for this unit. Mark this onto the unit you are going to draft logs onto. Remember, the dot indicates where the first log you draft onto the unit will lie and the arrow tells you the direction. Using a fine, black marker and a gridded ruler, draft a 1 cm (³/8 in) wide log onto the unit where indicated (Fig. 8). Now, working in the direction of the arrow, draft the next three outside logs. Continue drafting the logs until you have four logs on either side of the center shape, so you have sixteen logs and a center shape. If the unit has a particular color on certain sides these should be marked at this time, as well as the piecing order, if desired.

Unit B3: Repeat the above process for Unit B3, noting that the logs are drafted in a clockwise direction (Fig. 9).

Edge Triangle B1: The edge triangles have three logs on either side of the center. Draft the logs in the direction of the arrows.

Note: There is a definite difference between finished units drafted in metric and those drafted in imperial measurements. The centers of some of the units marked in inches will be bigger than those marked in centimetres. So be aware that if you use imperial measurements, the finished project will be slightly different in appearance.

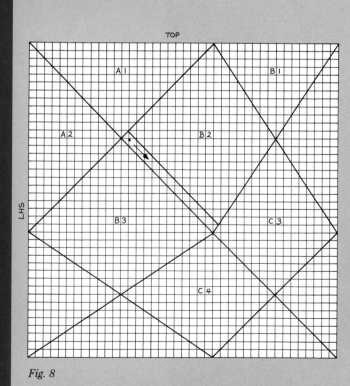

Fig. 8

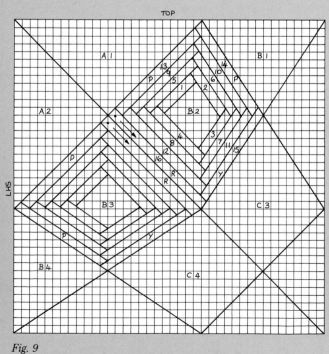

Fig. 9

Foundation Piecing

PREPARING AND MARKING THE FOUNDATION

1 Referring to the quilt project instructions, cut the required number of strips of the necessary width from the interfacing.

2 With your iron set on the wool/steam setting, carefully press the strips to pre-shrink them.

3 Cut the strips into the required-size squares, as instructed. These will be too big for some of the units, but don't worry about that – the excess is trimmed away after piecing.

4 As all the quilts in this book are pieced using under-pressed piecing, the units must be reversed before marking the foundations. If this is not done, the resulting quilt will be a mirror image of the original design. Under-pressed piecing is where all the sewing lines are marked onto the foundation, as opposed to top-pressed piecing where the fabric placement lines are marked. In under-pressed piecing, sew with the foundation on the top and the fabric underneath.

5 Place one of the drafted sheets of graph paper, with the drafted units face down, over a sheet of white cardboard on your work area. This reverses the design. You should be able to see the lines of the drafted logs and any identification marks quite clearly. Using the black pen, mark a dot at all four corners of the unit you are going to mark and transfer all the identification marks to this side of the paper. Mark a direction arrow at the top point of all units. This helps when placing the sewn unit onto the design wall.

6 Cut four pieces of tape, about 1 in (2.5 cm) long. Fold over one end of each strip to make a tab, which makes the tape easier to remove after marking.

7 Center a piece of interfacing over the unit you are going to trace. Lightly tape the four corners down with the tape. Make sure there is at least $1/2$ in (12 mm) of seam allowance extending beyond the outside marked lines of the unit.

8 Using a lead pencil and small plastic ruler, mark a dot at all four corners of the unit. Using the side of the pencil, not the point, trace over the four outside marked lines, extending the lines out through the corner dots to form crosses at the corners. This is where you will pin-match when joining the units together. Trace over the remaining log lines within the unit. Keep your pencil sharp.

9 Transfer all the identification marks and the direction arrow into the seam allowance, just outside the outer marked lines. This is very important as these are your orientation points when placing the completed units on the design wall and when joining groups. They must be close enough to the marked line so the unit identification number is not cut away when you trim the pieced unit. You can mark the piecing order and the color placement now, if you wish. If you mark the piecing order onto the drafted logs, do so lightly (see Sample 1).

10 Carefully, remove the traced unit from the graph paper. Check off the unit just marked on the photocopied layout.

11 Repeat the above steps for all the required units.

EDGE AND CORNER TRIANGLE UNITS

Most of the quilt projects have edge triangles. These are the triangles that are added to the outside edges to make the straight edge. Mark these in the same way as for the inner units. The best way to mark these is to keep the strip of interfacing in one piece. Lay one end over the required triangle and tape it in place. Mark the foundation, extending the lines out through the corner dots, forming crosses as before (see Sample 2). Cut the marked triangle off the strip leaving at least 1/2 in (12 mm) seam allowance extending beyond the outside marked lines. Repeat as many times as required.

The outside edges are identified by marking an * and the unit number just outside the outside edge marked line, in the seam allowance. Do this for every edge and corner triangle.

Some of the triangle units have the logs going right to the outside edges, thus having only two logs either side of the center shape – for example, 'Green Frames' on page 41. When this occurs, extend the marked sewing lines right out into the seam allowance as far as possible.

When making a project, it is sometimes easier to mark all the units that belong to one drafted area at the same time and then construct them. This way the units

are kept together, especially if it has a specific design as in 'Fireworks' on page 59. Study the quilt layout plan carefully. If the quilt is constructed in rows, work group by group down them, such as for 'Fanciful' on page 52 and 'Just a Little Bit' on page 66. For some quilts, I begin in the middle and work outward, piecing unit by unit, such as for 'Colors 2' on page 46. If the quilt is joined in four sections, work section by section.

Mark carefully and don't forget the identification marks and direction arrows. If you make a mistake here, you will find that your units are not correct when you go to sew them together. Check and double check. If you have trouble seeing the drafted lines through the interfacing, you can do one of two things: trace over all the lines before placing the foundation down; or when drafting, just mark the first log or two so you are going in the right direction, then turn the graph paper over and continue drafting. Trace over the first logs as well. However, you must be aware that if you do it this way, you will be drafting everything in reverse, so take extra care.

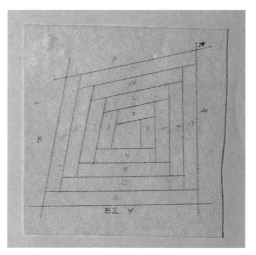

Sample 1: Marked foundation showing the identifying numbers, direction arrow and piecing order.

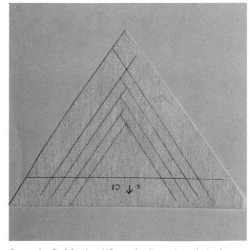

Sample 2: Marked foundation showing the extended sewing lines.

FOUNDATION PIECING

Because of the odd shapes of the group units and the size and shape of the logs, traditional methods of construction are not practical. Distortions tend to multiply rapidly. Foundation piecing allows you to achieve accuracy, especially if the design demands that certain points have to meet and some of the strips are very narrow.

All the quilt projects in this book are constructed using the foundation-piecing technique of under-pressed piecing. The unmarked side of the interfacing is the right side, the marked side is the wrong side. The fabric is sewn onto the unmarked side of the foundation material (right side) and it is underneath when sewing. You don't see the fabric while sewing. The marked sewing lines are on the top. This takes a bit of practice. There will be some shrinkage of the pieced units, but it will be uniform throughout the whole project.

Hints for Foundation Piecing

■ All the inside marked lines are sewing lines. The outside marked lines of the units are the lines used to join the units together. Do not sew fabric strips on the outside marked lines.

■ The first piece of fabric placed onto the foundation must face right side up. All the following pieces are placed right sides together.

■ When lining up the strips ready for sewing, have the line you are going to sew on in the vertical position, the area you are going to cover on your right and the bulk of the strip width on the left, with the seam allowance extending beyond the intended sewing line.

■ After sewing a strip in place, finger-press so it is firmly against the seam, then press with the iron. This avoids pleating which affects the log width, even if you have sewn on the lines accurately. Then turn the strip back and trim seam allowances. Reposition the strip in place.

■ When sewing the last three outside logs into position, note that the marked lines touch the outside marked sewing lines. Extend the stitching over these, into the seam allowance.

Foundation-piecing Method

1 Cut a section from the center fabric strip. Place this, right side down, beside the machine. Place the foundation over this with the marked side facing up, centering it so that the fabric is completely covering the marked center shape. Make sure that the fabric extends beyond all the marked sewing lines. You must have an adequate 1/4 in (6 mm) or more seam allowance extending on all sides and the top and bottom. Pin the piece in place (see Sample 3).

2 Hold the foundation up to a light source, with the marked side facing you. The

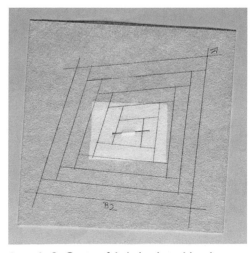

Sample 3: Center fabric is pinned in place.

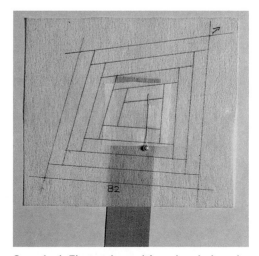

Sample 4: First strip positioned and pinned, ready for sewing.

marked line you are going to sew on should be in the vertical position. Place the strip of fabric for the first log over the center piece with the right sides facing. The bulk of the strip will hang down (see Sample 4). The top of the strip must extend 1/4 in (6 mm) beyond the intended sewing line of the log. You should be able to see the strip lined up through the interfacing. If you are not sure, pin the pieces along the sewing line and check.

If the unit is diamond-shaped, such as C4 in 'The Hot Line', then you must allow more seam allowance at the top or bottom of the strip. The same applies to edge and corner triangles. With these, leave plenty of seam allowance. If you don't, there will not be enough length to cover the area (see Samples 5a and 5b).

3 Sew the strip in place. Begin sewing one or two stitches before the marked line and sew one or two after it (see Sample 6).

4 After sewing, turn the unit over. Clip off all the threads and the excess strip 3/8 in (1 cm) beyond the end of the stitching. Finger-press, then press with the iron. Open the strip out and trim the seam allowance so you can clearly see the next parallel marked stitching line.

Hold the foundation up to a light source again and place the next strip into position. The bulk of the strip will hang down. You should be able to see the strip placement through the foundation. Sew, then trim the threads and the excess strip. Press, then trim the seam allowance.

5 Repeat the last steps until all the logs have been sewn into position. Remember to refer to the color placement guide to keep the fabrics in the correct order. Don't sew logs onto the outside marked lines – these are the seam joining lines for the units.

6 After the unit is assembled, stay-stitch around it, about 1/8 in (4 mm) from the outside marked line. Use the rotary cutting equipment to trim the edges of the unit, leaving a 3/8 in (1 cm) seam allowance extending all around it. If you trim the units now, it will not have to be done later (see Sample 7).

7 Edge and corner triangles are pieced in the same way. If you extended the marked lines for the logs over the outside marked line and into the seam allowance, make sure the strips extend this far as well (see Sample 8).

8 After completing a unit, pin it up on your design wall with the direction arrow at the top of the unit. Using a fluorescent marker, put a line through that particular unit on your photocopied quilt layout plan. This will help you to keep track of which units you have pieced and which are still to be sewn.

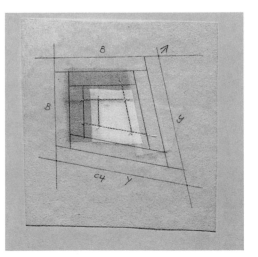

Sample 5a: A diamond-shaped unit with extra seam allowance.

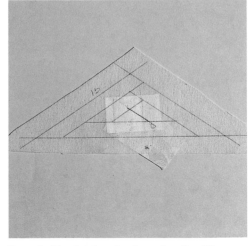

Sample 5b: A triangle-shaped unit with extra seam allowance.

Joining Units into Groups

All seams must be pressed open. This is very important, because it distributes the seam allowance bulk evenly across the quilt surface.

Don't reduce the stitch length on your machine. If you have to remove any stitching, do it carefully as the interfacing tears easily. The best way to remove stitching is to carefully cut every third or fourth stitch in the seam, then pull the pieces apart. The stitching will pop apart.

Some quilts are assembled in diagonal rows, others are assembled in four sections. Assembly plans, showing the joining sequences, are included for all the quilt projects. If you study the quilt layout plans carefully, you will notice that most of the seams for joining the rows and/or groups together are not straight seams. They form a zigzag effect. If the seam does zigzag the slightest bit from group to group or unit to unit, then it should be treated as if it were a set-in seam. That is, you must stop and start stitching exactly at the marked corner dots. If you don't, the quilt will be impossible to put together and will not lie flat. Because stitching in this way can be very awkward and frustrating when there is a lot of bulk involved, it is easiest to begin sewing at the outer edge and go one or two stitches past the first corner dot. Backstitch to the dot and continue sewing to the other end, stopping at the dot. Backstitch, then sew to

the end (see Sample 9). This way, if a seam allowance must be released, you only have to remove the first or last couple of stitches. The backstitching anchors the rest of the seam. I sew every seam in this manner throughout the whole construction process.

Before joining the units together in groups of four, join them into pairs. The pairs are then joined to form the group. Look for the straightest seam possible for the joining sequence. If you refer back to your original drafted units, you will be able to see if there is a straight seam in the group or not. Always sew the straightest seam last.

When you take the units off the design wall to join them together, unpin the top one and flip it face down over the one it is to be joined to. Roughly pin the two units together along the edge where you are going to sew. This way you do not sew the wrong edges together. (It's easily done!)

When joining two units together, pin match at the corner dots and use plenty of pins to hold them in place. Pin along the marked sewing line, matching the top and bottom (see Sample 10). When you have the units pinned together, the edges of some of them will not line up and will stick out at odd angles. Pull the pins out as you sew up to them. Press all the seams open.

Figure 11 shows the units being joined where there is a straight seam running through the middle. Join the units in the following

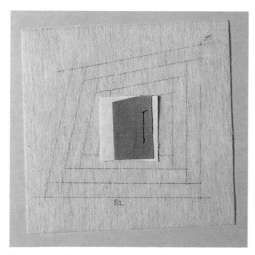

Sample 6: First log sewn in place and the excess trimmed off.

Sample 7: Finished unit, stay-stitched and trimmed.

sequence. A1 + A3 and A2 + A4. Sew these seams from outside edge to outside edge, then press the seams open. The remaining seam to join the group is straight. Sew from outside edge to outside edge, keeping the center seam allowances open.

The group shown in figure 12 has no straight seams running through the middle. Join B1 + B3 and B2 + B4, sewing from edge to edge. Press the seams open. The seam allowances that are at the center of the group must be released for it to lie flat. To do this, begin sewing at the outside edge and stop at the center dot, then backstitch. Make sure the seam allowances are out of the way. Release the few stitches in the seam allowances of the joined pairs as far as the stay-stitching. Turn the group around, pin, then begin sewing from the outside edge and stopping at the center dot. Press the seams open (see Samples 11 and 12).

As soon as you have joined a group, place it back on the wall. Because all the seams are pressed open there will only be one direction arrow visible. This is the top of the group.

Joining Groups to Form Rows or Sections

When working out the assembly sequence, I look for straight diagonal lines on the quilt plan that could divide the quilt into four sections. If the design has these, then I assemble the units into quarters or sections, join them into halves, then join the halves to form the top. This method makes handling the bulk of the quilt a lot easier.

If there are no obviously diagonal straight or semi-straight seams, the groups must be joined in rows, as in 'Fireworks' on page 59.

When joining the groups into rows, sew from outside edge to outside edge (see Sample 13). Pin-match at the corner dots and through the center seam allowance. Except for the end anchoring pins, pin along the matched sewing lines. Remember to backstitch at the dots at the outside corners of the groups, as some of the seam allowances will have to be released when you join the rows together. Sew straight through, keeping the middle seam allowances open and flat.

After joining two groups, pin them back up on the wall. Again, there will only be one direction arrow showing (see Sample 14).

If the quilt is assembled in four sections, refer to the assembly plan carefully. Some units will be joined into groups of four and others into groups of two. The same joining sequence as before applies here too.

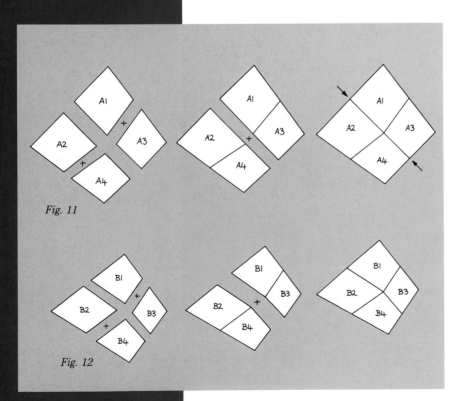

Fig. 11

Fig. 12

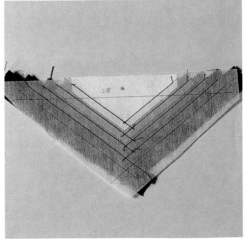

Sample 8: Pieced edge triangle showing extra fabric in the outside seam allowance.

Corner and Edge Triangles

The majority of the projects have corner and edge triangles to complete them. How these are joined to the units depends on how the units are to be joined together. Depending on the quilt design, the corner and side edge triangles can be attached in two different ways.

Group by group joining:

If the units are joined together to form groups, you will notice that there are odd units all around the edges that aren't included. These units are joined to the neighbouring edge triangles to form edge triangle sections (Figs. 13 and 14). After the groups have been joined into rows, these edge sections are joined to the ends to complete the rows. (See quilt layout plan for 'Just a Little Bit' on page 69)

Corner triangles:

The corner triangles are usually joined together to form corner units. These are joined to the quilt top after the other units have been assembled. If the quilt has been assembled in four sections, the corner triangles are sewn separately or as a corner unit to the adjacent groups or units, before the four sections are joined.

Joining Rows of Groups

To join rows of groups together, sew the rows of groups into pairs first, then join the pairs to make sections of rows. If you do

this, the last seam forming the quilt will have an equal amount of bulk in each half.

When joining the rows, you will be sewing only two unit groups together at a time, from corner dot to corner dot. Pin-match everything (corner dots, center seam allowances, keeping them flat, and marked sewing lines). Keep the seam allowances out of the way.

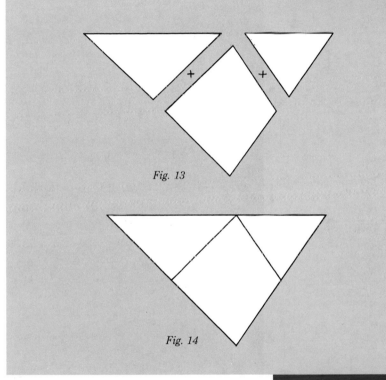

Fig. 13

Fig. 14

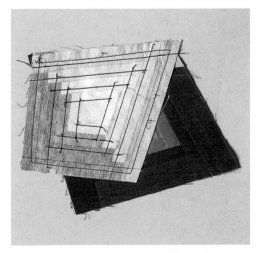

Sample 9: Two units joined with back-stitching at the corner dots.

Sample 10: Two units pinned together, ready to be sewn.

When pinning the rows together, lay the quilt onto a flat surface. The bulk of the quilt will lie at odd angles. Be very careful that loose seam allowances are pushed to one side when you come to the corners of groups. If you sew these down, the quilt will not lie flat.

Remember, a lot of the seams have to be treated as if they were 'set in', so seam allowances have to be released at the ends. Apart from the outside edges, sew from group corner dot to group corner dot, backstitching as you go. Start and end not quite one stitch short of the dots. This way you will not sew into the seam allowances. It will not leave a hole at the seam junction. Press the row-joining seam open after all groups are joined together. The seam allowances that were released will spiral.

Make sure you pin each section up on your wall in its correct position after sewing. The arrow you marked at the top of the units will ensure that they are the right way up. Pressing the seams open will mean that there will only be one direction arrow visible.

Some of the rows of groups can be joined together with a straight seam. Check the quilt layout plan to make doubly sure. If you are positive, then you can sew straight through a group junction with the seam allowances opened flat. On some of the joining diagrams, I have indicated with a small arrow the seams that have to be released.

Joining Four Sections

The method for joining sections together is the same as for the rows, except that you must follow the assembly plans carefully, as there is a definite piecing order. Most of the units are grouped into four or two and these are joined together to form groups of six. The edge triangles and odd units are joined to form groups of three. These are joined to the ends of the inner groups before the rows are joined together and are indicated on the assembly plans for each project.

Press the assembled quilt thoroughly, making sure all seam allowances are flat.

BORDERS

Some of the quilts in this book have a single narrow border. The pieced sections of the quilt tops are so heavy because of the foundation layer that a wide unpieced border tends to ripple. I like to keep borders to about 2 in (5 cm) wide. The exceptions are 'Cabins in the Woods' on page 24 and 'Fanciful' on page 52. The borders of these two quilts have been machine-quilted.

If you don't want to add borders, you can just add binding directly onto the edges.

If you wish to add a border that is wider than $3^1/2$ in (9 cm), I recommend that you also attach the border strips to interfacing. Baste the layers together firmly and stay-stitch all edges. This will help to avoid rippling.

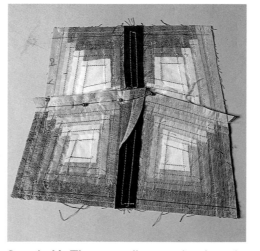

Sample 11: The seam allowance is released and the second seam is pinned.

Sample 12: The back of a sewn group showing the released seam allownces.

The fabric amounts given for the borders in these quilt projects are generous and the instructions give cutting measurements that include seam allowances and extra length at the ends.

Cutting and Attaching Borders

1. Cut the border strips as instructed.
2. On one long side of each border strip, mark a 3/8 in (1 cm) seam line with the chalk pencil.
3. Measure the quilt vertically through the center, from the outside marked lines on the foundations. Pin-mark this measurement onto two of the strips. You should have extra fabric extending at both ends of the pin marks.
4. Matching the pins, fold two of the strips in half to find the center. Pin-mark. Fold the strips again and pin-mark them into quarters.
5. Fold the quilt in half. Place pins through the outside marked corners of the top and bottom units, at the dot. Holding the pins firmly, locate the center and pin-mark it. Fold the quilt again into quarters and pin-mark on both sides of the quilt.
6. Pin a border strip to one side of the quilt, matching the pin marks. Pin the border to the quilt at about 1 in (2.5 cm) intervals, pinning along the marked sewing lines. With the border strip underneath, sew the border to the quilt, from the outside edge to the outside edge. Trim the seam allowance to 1/4 in (7.5 mm). Press the seam toward the border. Repeat for the other side of the quilt.
7. Using the rotary cutter and ruler, trim the excess border extending beyond the top and bottom edges of the quilt, even with the quilt edge. Using the chalk pencil and a ruler, extend the sewing lines along the top and bottom of the quilt into the sewn borders. This gives you a straight line to sew on (Fig. 15).
8. Repeat the above steps for the top and bottom borders, using the remaining two strips. This time, measure horizontally from the outside edges of the borders.

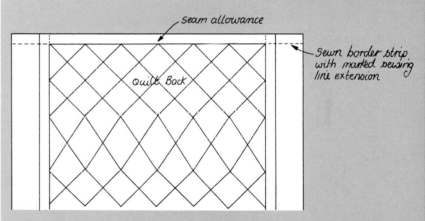

Fig. 15

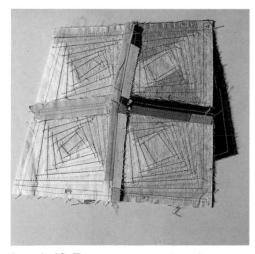

Sample 13: Two groups sewn together.

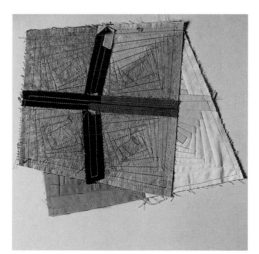

Sample 14: Two joined groups with the one remaining arrow visible.

Assembly

BACKING FABRIC

The majority of the quilt projects in this book have been tied. Because of this there is no need for the backing and batting to extend more than 3 in (7.5 cm) all around the quilt edges. This amount has been allowed for in the fabric requirements for each project. If you want to add borders to any of the quilts to make them larger, use the layout plans to calculate the additional fabric required. Remember, you will also need to have larger backing and batting pieces.

If you have to join the backing, press the seam open and have it running down the length of the quilt, through the center. Don't forget to remove the selvages.

BATTING

The piece of batting needs to be the same size as the backing fabric. If you change the given amount for the backing fabric, change the batting size by the same amount.

I recommend that you use a very thin batting for the quilts. Pellon is excellent. It is 48 in (122 cm) wide, which is wide enough for every project in this book. Pellon gives the quilts a flat look and it is easy to tie through. Remember, there is an extra layer in the quilt because of the permanent foundation material, so avoid a high-loft batting. If you have to join the batting, butt the edges together and join them using a large zigzag stitch.

LAYERING

Spread the backing, wrong side facing up, on the floor or a large flat surface. Smooth out any wrinkles and have it as straight as possible. Use masking tape to secure it, if you are working on a table, or pins, if you are working on the carpet. I like to work on the carpet because it tends to hold the layers firmly, without shifting.

Spread the batting out centering it over the backing, making it as flat and wrinkle-free

as possible. Tape or pin this as for the backing, to hold it securely in place.

Place the pressed top, right side facing up, over the layers and smooth it gently from the center outward. Pin or tape this in position, as well. If you joined the backing fabric, fold the quilt in half to locate the center and pin-match at the top and bottom. Now, match these pins with the backing seam.

Pin-baste the layers together with long quilter's pins in or near the centers of every second unit. Begin in the center and work toward the sides, then up and down across the quilt. Pin around the edges of the quilt, just beyond the border seam. After pinning, run a row of thread-basting around the border, just beyond the outside seam line and again halfway between the outside edges of the borders and the border seam. For quilts without borders, thread-baste around the outside edge, beyond the stay-stitching, and again about 1/2 in (12 mm) inside the stay-stitching. Remove the pins or tape fixing the layers to the work surface. If the units were trimmed after piecing, there should be a 3/8 in (1 cm) seam allowance all around.

TYING

All the quilts in this book, except one, have been tied. Even though machine-quilting adds texture and interest to the surface, I like the quilt design to be dominant. Tying at the major seam allowance intersections on the back holds the layers together firmly, leaving the front smooth. If the quilt has a narrow border, I sometimes machine-stitch 'in-the-ditch' after tying. Turn the pin-basted quilt over onto a flat hard surface.

Anchor the layers on the back of the quilt at large seam allowance intersections. This is usually where the group joins lie. You can actually feel them through the layers. If in doubt, take a peek at the front first.

Thread your needle with six strands of embroidery floss, about 40 in (102 cm) long. Beginning in the center, use your fingers to locate the centermost seam intersection. Take a stitch no bigger than 1/4 in (6 mm) through the backing, batting and seam allowance bulk. Do not let the needle pierce the front. Pull the thread through, leaving yourself enough length to tie with – about 2 in (5 cm). You may need a pair of pliers to do this.

Cut the floss and tie off the ends. If you don't want the ends to show, leave some extra length when cutting the floss and sew them through into the quilt layers after tying. Allow extra embroidery floss for this.

Continue tying, working from the center out to the sides, then work from the center up and across to the top, then down and across to the bottom. After you have finished tying, turn the quilt over and remove all the pins.

MACHINE-QUILTING

If you want to machine-quilt, pin-baste first, then thread-baste the layers together, trying not to have any threads in the intended quilting path. Because of the quilt thickness, you will need to use a heavier needle for the quilting (a number 90 or a denim needle). If you use a smaller needle, you will have missed or skipped stitches. Whatever size needle you use, you may still end up with holes showing on the surface of the quilt. Try to avoid quilting in the areas where there are unit joins, as you will have up to eight thicknesses to sew through.

If you are going to quilt a pattern in a border, don't make it too heavy or the quilt will not hang well and the edges will ripple. An open meandering pattern, using free-motion quilting and a darning foot, is enough to hold the layers together ('Fanciful', page 52). 'Cabins in the Woods' (page 24) has been machine-quilted in the pieced areas, in the border seam and in the borders. The pieced area was tied before it was machine-quilted.

When machine-quilting in-the-ditch, stitch on top of the border seam, after the pieced area has been tied and before the borders are quilted. This prevents the quilting pulling stitches from the tied area and causing puckers.

BINDING

Because most of these quilts are intended to hang on a wall, all the bindings are cut on the straight grain and are a single layer.

The binding width for all the quilts is the same. They are cut 1 3/4 in (4.5 cm) wide and are sewn to the quilt using a 3/8 in (1 cm) seam allowance. When they are folded to the back and hand-sewn down, they finish at 3/8 in (1 cm) wide. After turning the binding strip to the back, generously turn the raw edge under. Make sure the edges of the quilt layers are right in the fold, completely filling the binding.

Use the same method for attaching the bindings as you did for the borders, attaching the sides first, then the top and bottom. Whipstitch the side bindings down, before attaching the top and bottom bindings. When sewing the top and bottom bindings, leave an extra 1 in (2.5 cm) at the ends to turn over and cover the raw ends of the side bindings. Turn this extra length over the corners before whipstitching the sides.

ROD POCKET

Measure the width of the quilt and add 3/4 in (2 cm) to this length. Cut a strip of fabric, 8 in (20 cm) wide by this measurement. Hem the two short edges with a 3/8 in (1 cm) hem.

Fold the strip in half, bringing the two long edges, wrong sides together, and sew a 1/4 in (7.5 mm) seam. Fold the pocket so that the seam allowances are about 3/4 in (2 cm) down from the fold. Place the pocket on the back of the quilt with the seam allowance against the backing and the folded edge butting up against the bottom edge of the binding. Pin the pocket in place and blind-stitch this edge down.

Roll the top fold of the pocket up to the top of the binding so it is not seen from the front. Pin it in place. Pin the resulting bottom fold of the pocket to the quilt back and blind-stitch it in place.

Because most of these quilts are tied on the back, not quilted, make sure you actually catch some of the seam allowances of the pieced areas as you sew the bottom fold. This stops the rod pocket from dragging the back of the quilt.

LABELING YOUR QUILT

It is important to name and date your quilt for future reference. The label can be as plain or as fancy as you like. It can be embroidered by hand or by machine, or written with a waterproof marker.

Equipment

The equipment described here is required for all the projects in this book. You will be referred back to this list in the instructions for each project.

Access to a photocopier is important. I recommend that you photocopy and enlarge the quilt layout plan for the project you are going to make. This way you can cross off units as you make them, without damaging the pages in the book.

Basic supplies
■ Sewing machine in good working order. Look after it. It should be cleaned and oiled regularly. Refer to your manual, if you are in any doubt. After oiling, make sure you sew on scraps to get rid of all the excess oil. For straight machine-quilting, a walking foot on your machine is desirable. For free-motion quilting, use a darning foot and lower the feed dogs. Some machines have a small metal plate that fits over the feed dogs. If you can't lower the feed dogs and there is no metal plate available, tape a piece of thin card in place, but first cut a small opening for the needle.
■ Sewing machine needles (Universal 80/12 and 90/14). Needles need to be changed frequently. The life of a needle is really limited to eight hours sewing. For machine-quilting in pieced areas, use a Universal 90/14. For quilting in the borders, I use a Universal 80/12. Experiment to find a needle that suits you and your machine.
■ Strong sewing needle with an eye big enough to thread six strands of embroidery floss, for tying the quilt. A curved upholstery needle works well for this purpose.
■ Small pair of pliers
■ Tape measure
■ Needle and thread for basting
■ Scissors
■ Seam ripper
■ Straight pins
■ Long quilters' pins for pin-basting
■ Chalk pencil or wheel
■ Rotary cutting equipment, including a self-healing mat, and a rotary cutter
■ Rulers, ideally a 6^1/2 in × 12^1/2 in and 6^1/2 in × 24 in (16.5 cm × 32 cm and 16.5 cm × 61 cm)
■ Vertical work space, for pinning the work up during construction. If you don't have a suitable 'pin-up' wall, a sheet or piece of flannel pinned to a curtain works well.
■ Steam iron, located as close to your machine as possible. You will be pressing as much as sewing.
■ Thread in a neutral color, such as cream, grey or beige, for all the foundation piecing, and matching thread for joining the units and groups and for the borders and the bindings. I use Coats Duet which is a poly/cotton.
■ Foundation material, such as a medium-weight non-fusible interfacing that is 40 in (102 cm) wide. Don't use one that is too light, as this will cause a lot of shrinkage and puckering, or too heavy, as it is hard to see through and is unwieldy.

Unit Drafting and Foundation Marking Equipment
Every project in this book requires the following equipment for drafting and marking the necessary units.
■ Pad of 11 in × 17 in (A3) graph paper, marked in ^{1}/4 in (5 mm) divisions
■ Gridded ruler, measuring 2 in × 18 in (4 cm × 40 cm) and marked in ^{1}/16 in (2 mm) increments. The metric version is a pattern grading ruler and is available with red or black markings. If you are working with imperial measurements, use the long, thin quilter's ruler that is 2 in × 18 in.
■ Large sheet of white heavy-weight cardboard
■ Fine-point, black, felt-tipped marker pen, such as an Artline no 2
■ Fluorescent marker for crossing off the units on the layout plans when they have been pieced
■ Black, lead pencil; the Staedtler Tradition 110 HB gives a good dark line, or use a mechanical pencil
■ Pencil sharpener
■ Small plastic ruler, 8 in (20 cm) long
■ Magic tape or removable Scotch tape. Don't substitute ordinary sticky tape – it does not peel off easily and will tear the interfacing and the paper.

Fabric

I love to use strong, bold colors in my quilts and for this reason I mostly use solids, either in color gradations – shades of one color, light to dark, or in color runs; for example, yellow-orange-red-burgundy. The majority of the projects in this book are constructed using solid fabrics which give a crisp, bold look. Print fabrics can be used, but take care with the selection because a definite contrast is needed to make the designs work.

Where possible, use one hundred percent cotton fabrics, washed, then ironed when they are still damp. If you don't wash your fabrics, at least do a test to see if they run. There is nothing more disheartening than to wash a quilt and have the dyes run and ruin it.

Some of my quilts include polyester and other blends to achieve the colors I want to use. This is fine for the more experienced, but I recommend that you use cottons to begin with. Poly/cotton blends can be used, but be aware that they tend to bounce back after pressing and could cause pleating.

Once you become familiar with the foundation piecing technique, any type of fabric can be used from woollens to silks. Furnishing fabrics can also be used quite successfully – some of the colors and patterns can really add spice to the finished quilt. Be aware that if you combine fabrics of different weights, the shrinkage that does occur can be unpredictable. Some units will shrink unevenly and joining them together could be a problem, so try to work with fabrics of similar weights.

Color and Value

When working with color gradations or color runs for a quilt design, be careful that the step between each pair of fabrics is sufficient. If they are very close in value, from a distance the fabrics will read as one color (see Samples 1–3).

When planning the fabrics for a project, make a mock-up of those you think will work. Small pieces, 1 in x 2 in (2.5 cm x 5 cm) are big enough. Pin them on your design wall and stand back. You will soon know if a particular fabric is right or wrong. Fabric contrasts can look good close up, but at a distance they may bleed into one another. Be adventurous – try combinations you would not normally use. If you have trouble using one particular color, then force yourself to include it. You could be surprised.

Fabric Quantity

It's very hard to accurately estimate fabric amounts for the quilts. The amounts given for each quilt project in this book are generous and are based on 44 in (112 cm) wide fabrics. Some solid fabrics are narrower than this, so make sure you check before you buy. You may have to purchase extra length. I like to use curtain fabric on the back of my quilts. These fabrics are a lot wider so you don't have to buy so much. The length of the quilt plus 6 in (15 cm) is usually sufficient.

When cutting strips from yardage (metrage), only cut one strip and make up a unit. If you are satisfied, then cut more. I cut strips as I need them. If I find that a color isn't working, I haven't wasted a lot of fabric – only one strip. This is the most economical way of working.

When you start a project and you have worked out the particular fabrics you want to use, cut small pieces of them and attach them, in order, onto the photo-copied layout plan.

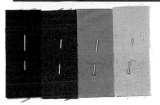
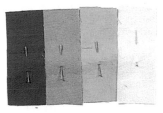
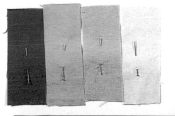

Sample 1 (top): A color run with definite steps.
Sample 2 (middle): Definite steps between the fabrics.
Sample 3 (bottom): Colors are too close in value.

YOU WILL NEED

Note: Fabric quantities are calculated for 44 in (112 cm) wide fabric. The specified amounts are generous.

- 3 yd (2.7 m) of a multi-colored print fabric for the units and borders
- 16 in (40 cm) of a dark green fabric for the unit centers and bindings
- 4 in (10 cm) each of twenty light fabrics

Note: I used all off-white and cream fabrics, repeating them several times. To do this, you will need 8 in (20 cm) of at least eight to ten off-white or cream fabrics.

- 4 in (10 cm) of twenty different medium-to-dark fabrics
- 2³/4 yd (2.5 m) of medium-weight interfacing
- 1¹/2 yd (1.4 m) of fabric for the backing
- 1¹/2 yd (1.4 m) of Pellon batting
- basic sewing and drafting equipment
- neutral-colored thread for piecing
- thread to match the border fabric
- one skein of embroidery floss to match or contrast with the backing fabric
- matching or contrasting thread for machine-quilting

Cabins in the Woods

This small quilt is a warm-up exercise. The grid that it is based on is not distorted, but the units within each group are. There are two different groups, X and Y. Each is made up of four identically drafted units, which are rotated ninety degrees to form the pattern.

You only need to draft the logs for tracing the foundations into one unit of each group. Where all four units meet in the center of the group place a symbol (*). This is an orientation mark to help you place the units in the correct place after sewing. When marking the foundations, make sure that you copy all the identifying marks. Mark each unit A or B. The B unit will not fit into a Group X and an A unit will not fit into Group Y.

It is also a good idea to lightly mark the fabric placement and the piecing order on the first few units, if you are not confident.

The design of this quilt relies on specific fabric placement. In each group, all of the units have the outside logs in the same fabric. The remaining logs that come together in the center are made from two contrasting fabrics. The center shape of each unit is also the same dark fabric.

Finished size: 37¹/2 in × 44¹/2 in (95 cm × 113 cm)

DRAFTING

See the Quilt Layout Plan on page 29. Place a sheet of cardboard on the table. Draw up two 8 in (20 cm) squares on a sheet of graph paper. Label one square Group X and the other one Group Y.

For Group X:

1 Working in a clockwise direction, divide all four sides of the square into two sections at 3 in (8 cm) and 5 in (12 cm) increments. Going from dot to dot, rule in the lines to divide the square into four units (Fig. 1).

2 Study the diagram for the starting position and direction for drafting the logs. There are four logs on either side of the center shape. They all spiral in a clockwise direction from the same starting point. As all the units are the same, you only need to draft the logs onto one unit. Make sure you mark the * in the center corner. Label the unit A (Fig. 2).

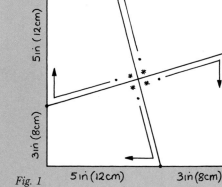

Fig. 1

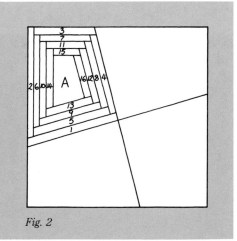

Fig. 2

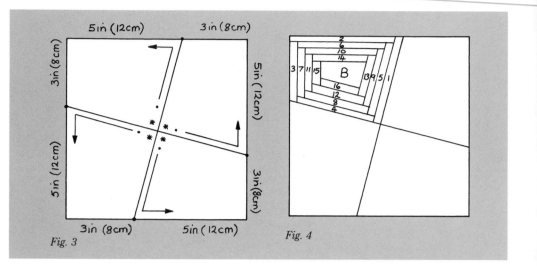

Fig. 3

Fig. 4

3 Begin drafting 3/8 in (1 cm) wide logs, starting at the dot and working in the direction of the arrow. Refer to the detailed instructions for "Drafting the Units" on pages 6–10.

For Group Y:

1 Divide each of the four sides of the second square into two sections at 5 in (12 cm) and 3 in (8 cm) increments (Fig. 3).

2 Refer to the group diagram (above) and draft the logs. They start in the center of the group but spiral in a counter-clockwise direction. Begin drafting 3/8 in (1 cm) wide logs onto one unit, starting at the dot and going in the direction of the arrow. Make sure you mark the * in the center corner. Label the unit B (Fig. 4).

MARKING THE FOUNDATIONS

Note: Refer to the detailed instructions for "Preparing and Marking the Foundation" on page 11.

1 Turn the graph paper over so the marked side is face down on the cardboard. Mark a dot at the four corners of the log drafted units. Transfer all identifying marks. There is no need to re-mark the logs, as you should be able to see the lines. Trace over the logs if

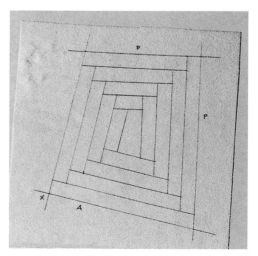

Sample 1: Marked unit A with fabric placement, piecing order and identifying number in the seam allowance.

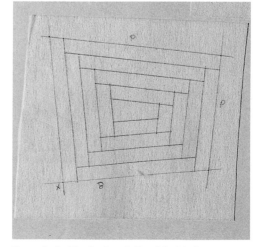

Sample 2: Marked unit B with fabric placement, piecing order and identifying number in the seam allowance.

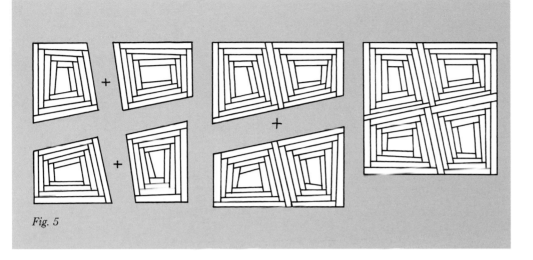

Fig. 5

you think you are going to have trouble seeing them. I suggest that you mark the piecing order lightly onto the logs. The shortest log being number 1, the longest being number 16. Transfer these lightly to the foundations after marking. They will help to keep the fabric placement correct. After constructing a few units you will no longer need them.

2 Cut the interfacing into fourteen strips, each 6 in (15 cm) wide. Press the strips to pre-shrink them.

3 Cut each of the strips into six 6 in (15 cm) squares. These will be way too big; the excess will be trimmed away later.

4 You will need forty unit As and forty unit Bs. To begin with, just mark four unit As, label them A and mark the *. After marking, pin the four units together so they stay as a group. Now mark four unit Bs and pin them together in the same way (see Samples 1 and 2).

CUTTING THE FABRIC

1 From the border fabric, cut four 4 1/2 in (11.5 cm) wide strips across the width of the fabric. Set them aside.

2 From the binding fabric, cut the following:
■ five 1 3/4 in (4.5 cm) wide strips across the width of the fabric. Set them aside. The extra strip is for making up the required length for the side bindings;
■ twenty 1 in (2.5 cm) wide strips. Cut more as needed.

3 From the dark fabric for the unit centers, cut one 1 1/4 in (3.5 cm) wide strip. Cut more as needed.

4 From the contrasting fabrics, make mock-ups of twenty different groups of one dark and one light fabric. Tape them down onto the back of the photocopied layout plan or pin them onto your design wall. Select a pair and cut two 1 in (2.5 cm) wide strips from each.

CONSTRUCTION

Note: Refer to the detailed instructions for "Foundation Piecing" on page 13. I suggest that you piece groups alternately; this way you can see the design forming.

1 Study the picture of Samples 3 and 4 for Group Y on page 28. The centers are both dark green and there are two variations. Two of the units in the group are pieced beginning with the light contrasting fabric and the other two begin with the dark contrasting fabric. Logs numbered 2, 3, 6, 7, 10, 11, 14 and 15 are pieced using the print fabric. These are the outside logs of the units.

2 Piece four units for Group Y, making two of each variation.

3 After constructing a unit, use the rotary cutting equipment to trim excess fabric and interfacing from around the outside edges, leaving a 3/8 in (1 cm) seam allowance extending beyond the outside marked lines.

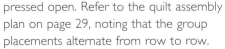

4 Join the four units together to form Group Y (Fig. 5). All the seams are straight. Pin-match the corners and use at least two pins along the sewing line to stop any movement. Sew from the outside edge to the outside edge. Press the seams open.

5 Continue to piece the remaining groups in the same manner. Place the groups up on the display wall, as you finish them. When you have constructed all the groups and have a pleasing arrangement, you can begin to put the quilt together.

ASSEMBLY

Note: This quilt is assembled in straight rows. All the seam allowances should be pressed open. Refer to the quilt assembly plan on page 29, noting that the group placements alternate from row to row.

1 Pin-match the corners and along marked sewing lines, then join the groups together to form rows.

2 Join the rows together to form the quilt top. Use as many pins as you wish to hold the rows together. Pull them out just as you get to them.

BORDERS

Note: Refer to the detailed instructions for "Borders" on page 18.

1 Prepare the pre-cut border strips. Sew the borders to the sides of the quilt. Trim the top and bottom even with the

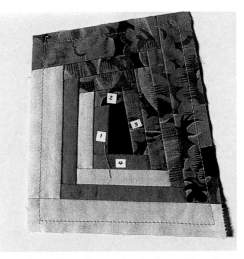

Sample 3: Pieced unit, beginning with a dark contrasting fabric.

Sample 4: Pieced unit, beginning with a light contrasting fabric.

Sample 5: Completed Group X.

Sample 6: Completed Group Y.

quilt edges. Extend the sewing lines out into the borders to give a line to sew on when attaching the top and bottom borders.

2 Repeat for the top and bottom borders of the quilt.

LAYERING

Note: Refer to the detailed instructions for "Layering" on page 20.

Assemble the three layers of the quilt. Pin-baste the layers together.

TYING

Note: Refer to the detailed instructions for "Tying" on pages 20–21.

On the back, tie the quilt at all the group center intersections and at the group row join seams.

QUILTING

Note: Refer to the detailed instructions for "Machine-quilting" on page 21.

1 Using a darning foot on the machine, free-motion quilt a meandering design in the print fabric areas of the pieced area. Avoid the large seam intersections.

2 Quilt in the ditch in the border seam.

3 Quilt your desired pattern in the borders, if you wish. This quilt has borders that are 3½ in (9 cm) finished width, so the design should be no wider than 3 in (7.5 cm). If the design is any wider than that, it will be cut off when the quilt edges are trimmed. Don't make the quilting too heavy, as it will cause the borders to ripple; make it just enough to hold the layers together.

BINDING

Refer to the detailed instructions for "Binding", "Rod Pocket", and "Labeling Your Quilt" on page 21.

1 Trim the edges of the quilt layers, leaving a 3½ in (9 cm) wide border.

2 Baste around the outside edge, if you have cut away the outer basting, to stop movement when the binding is attached.

3 Using the pre-cut binding strips, measure and apply the binding in the same manner as for the borders. You will need to cut one strip in half and sew one half to two other strips to achieve the length required for the side bindings. These will be way too long, so trim the excess after sewing. Turn the binding strips to the back of the quilt and stitch down.

4 Repeat for the top and bottom bindings with the two remaining strips. Leave 2 in (5 cm) extra for turning around the corners.

5 Sew a label to the back and a rod pocket for hanging if desired.

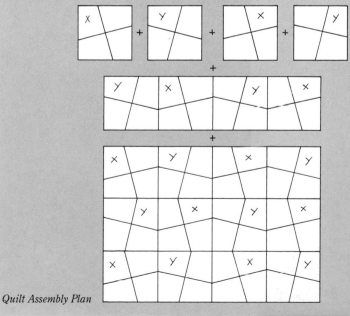

Quilt Layout Plan

Quilt Assembly Plan

YOU WILL NEED
Note: Fabric quantities are calculated for 44 in (112 cm) wide fabric. The specified amounts are generous.

- 12 in (30 cm) each of royal blue, navy blue, cream and yellow fabric
- 18 in (45 cm) of medium blue fabric
- 16 in (40 cm) of light blue fabric
- 14 in (36 cm) of rusty, red-orange fabric
- 14 in (36 cm) of orange fabric
- 8 in (20 cm) each of bright burgundy and dark burgundy fabric
- 16 in (40 cm) of black-and-white-striped fabric for inner border and unit piecing
- 12 in (30 cm) of black-and-white-print fabric for the unit centers
- 24 in (60 cm) of dark navy blue fabric for the outer borders and binding
- basic sewing and drafting equipment
- neutral-colored thread for the piecing
- matching thread for joining the units and the borders
- navy blue thread for machine-quilting
- number 90 machine needle
- 2 yd (1.9 m) of medium-weight interfacing
- chalk pencil
- 1¹/₈ yd (1.1 m) of fabric for the backing
- 1¹/₈ yd (1.1 m) of Pellon batting

Opposing Forces

This small quilt uses the same drafting directions as 'Cabins in the Woods' on page 24. It is a great example of how fabric choice and placement can achieve two totally different quilts from the same pattern.

Two color runs are used throughout this quilt: blue to cream and burgundy to yellow. The pattern is formed through the use of a black-and-white-striped fabric in the outside logs of some of the units. Study the coloured diagrams and Samples carefully as there are fabric variations within the groups. Photocopy the quilt layout plan.

Finished size: 35³/4 in (91 cm) square

FABRIC PLACEMENT
You will need to draft logs onto two units of each group (A and B), as there are two variations of fabric placements for each one.

Group A (Fig. 1)
Variation 1
Two units are pieced beginning with cream in the first (shortest) log. Logs 13 and 16 are royal blue; logs 14 and 15 are bright burgundy. The piecing order is as follows: the first round of logs is cream, yellow, yellow, cream; the second round is pale blue, orange, orange, pale blue etc. (See Sample 1 on page 32.)

Variation 2
Two units are pieced beginning with yellow in the first (shortest) log. Logs 13 and 16 are black-and-white-striped; logs 14 and 15 are royal blue. The piecing order is as follows: the first round of logs is yellow, cream, cream, yellow; the second round is orange, pale blue, pale blue, orange etc. (See Sample 2 on page 32.)

Group B (Fig. 2)
The variations are the same as for Group A, but substitute dark blue for royal blue and dark burgundy for bright burgundy. The units have the same piecing order as Group A. (See Samples 3 and 4 on page 32.)

DRAFTING
Note: Refer to the detailed instructions for "Drafting" on pages 6–10. See the Quilt Layout Plan on page 35.

Group A
1 Working in a clockwise direction, divide all four sides of the square into two sections at 3 in (8 cm) and 5 in (12 cm) increments. Going from dot to dot, rule in the lines to divide the square into four units.
2 Study the drafting diagram for Group A on the quilt layout plan. Determine the starting position and the direction for

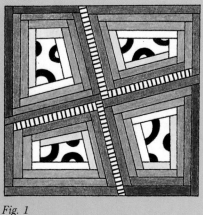
Fig. 1

Fig. 2

drafting in the logs and identification numbers for Variations 1 and 2. The logs all spiral in a clockwise direction from the same starting point. Draft 3/8 in (1 cm) wide logs onto the two unit variations, starting at the dot and working in the direction of the arrow. There are four logs on either side of the center. Mark the * in the center corners and label the units (Fig. 3). Mark the piecing order onto the logs. Mark the fabric placement variations.

Group B

1 Working in a clockwise direction, divide each of the four sides of the second square into two sections at 5 in (12 cm) and 3 in (8 cm) increments.

Work in the same way as for Group A, refer to the drafting diagram for Group B. Draft 3/8 in (1 cm) wide logs onto two units for Variations 1 and 2. They start in the center of the group and spiral counter-clockwise. After drafting the logs, mark the identification numbers and the piecing order (Fig. 4). Mark the fabric placement variations.

MARKING THE FOUNDATIONS

Note: Refer to the detailed instructions for "Preparing and Marking the Foundation" on page 11.

1 Turn the graph paper over so the marked side is face down on the cardboard. Note that everything is reversed. Make a dot at the four corners of the two drafted units for each group. Transfer all the identifying numbers, piecing order and fabric placement.

Sample 1: Group A, variation 1.

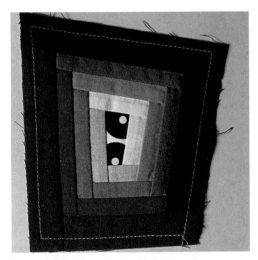

Sample 2: Group A, variation 2.

Sample 3: Group B, variation 1.

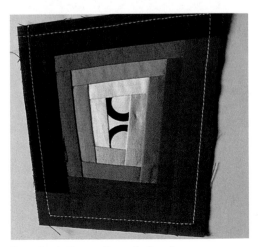

Sample 4: Group B, variation 2.

2 Cut the interfacing into eleven 6 in (15 cm) wide strips. Cut the strips into sixty-four 6 in (15 cm) squares. These will be way too big, but the excess is trimmed after piecing. Mark the foundations group by group. Make sure they are labeled correctly with all the identifying numbers, piecing order and fabric placement. After marking a group, pin the four units together ready for piecing. You will need sixteen each of Variation 1 and Variation 2 for group A, and sixteen each of Variation 1 and Variation 2 for group B, giving you eight each of groups A and B.

CUTTING FABRIC

Begin by cutting a 1¼ in (3 cm) wide strip from all of the fabrics. Cut more as required.

PIECING

Note: Refer to the detailed instructions for "Foundation Piecing" on page 13 and the order of piecing shown in figures 3 and 4.

1 Construct four units for a Group A, two of each variation. Using rotary cutting equipment, trim the edges of the units, leaving a ⅜ in (1 cm) seam allowance extending all around them.

2 After piecing, lay out the units in their correct order (Figs 5 and 6). Take care that all the * marks should be in the center of the group.

3 Pin-match the corners at the marked dots, then pin again about halfway along the marked line. Sew the units together into pairs, from outside edge to outside edge (Figs 7 and 8). Press all the seam allowances open.

4 Pin the pairs together, matching the corners and the center seam junction. Keep the seam allowance open. Place pins along the marked line as before. Sew. Press the seam open (Figs 9 and 10).

5 Make the remainder of the groups for the quilt in this way. Piece the groups alternately so you can see the design forming. You will need eight each of Groups A and Group B.

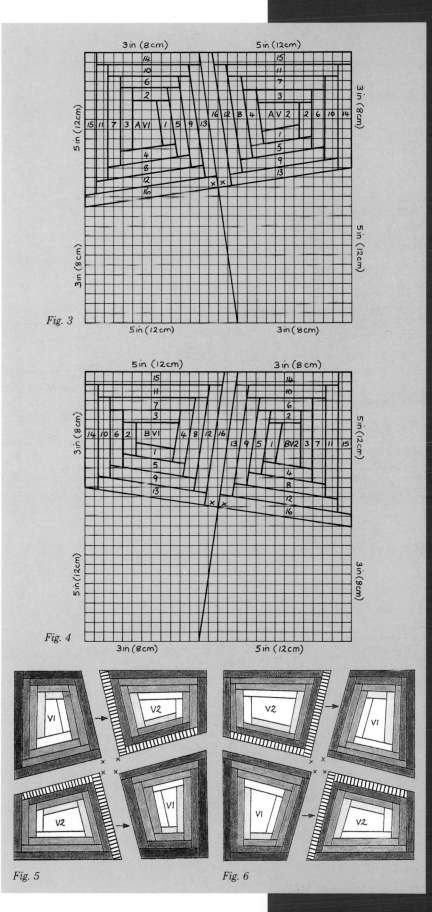

Fig. 3

Fig. 4

Fig. 5

Fig. 6

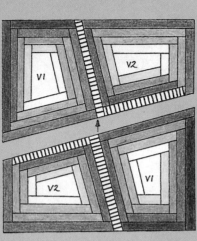

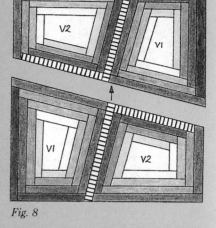

Fig. 7

Fig. 8

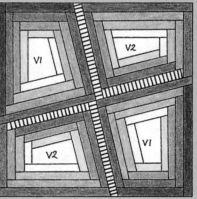

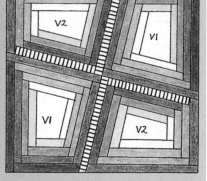

Fig. 9

Fig. 10

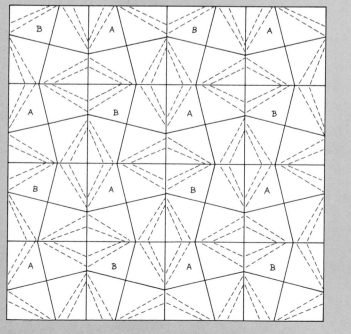

Fig. 11

ASSEMBLY

1 Assemble the quilt top, referring to the Quilt Assembly Plan on page 35. The groups alternate in each row. The first row begins with a Group B, the second row begins with a Group A and so on. Join the groups into rows, pin-matching the corner dots and along the seam lines. Sew from outside edge to outside edge. Press all the seams open.

2 Using plenty of pins, join the rows together to form the quilt top. Press all the seams open.

BORDERS

1 Using the black-and-white-striped fabric, cut four 1 1/2 in (4 cm) wide strips across the fabric width.

2 Mark a 3/8 in (1 cm) seam allowance along one long edge of all the strips.

3 Referring to the detailed instructions for "Borders" on pages 18–19, attach the inner borders. Trim the seam allowances to 1/4 in (7.5 mm) after sewing. Press the seams outward.

4 Using the rotary cutter, trim the inner borders to 3/4 in (2 cm) wide, to give you a nice straight edge.

5 Cut four 3 1/2 in (9 cm) wide strips across the fabric width from the outer border fabric.

6 Measuring and quartering as for the inner borders, attach the outer borders using a 1/4 in (7.5 mm) seam allowance.

LAYERING

Note: Refer to the detailed instructions for "Layering" on page 20.

1 Layer the backing, batting, and quilt top together on a flat surface.

2 Pin-baste thoroughly, using long quilter's pins. Avoid safety pins as they can damage the quilt top because of the extra thickness. Begin in the middle of the quilt and place a pin in the center of every group unit. Place pins in the narrow inner border, about 2 in (5 cm) apart. Pin the edges of the borders.

MACHINE-QUILTING

Note: Only mark small areas of your quilting design at a time, as the chalk will wear off. When quilting, work from the center to the outside edge. Refer to the detailed instructions for "Machine-quilting" on page 21.

1 Using the chalk wheel or pencil, and the ruler, mark the quilting design, as shown in figure 11.

2 Fold the quilt so the marked section is visible. Place this part under the machine and begin quilting, using a walking foot if you have one and the number 90 needle. Pull out each anchoring pin when you get to it. Mark and quilt all the appropriate sections.

3 Quilt in-the-ditch on both sides of the narrow inner border.

4 Trim the outer borders (including the backing and wadding) to 2¹/2 in (7 cm) wide.

FINISHING

Note: Refer to the detailed instructions for "Binding", "Rod Pocket", and "Labeling your Quilt" on page 21.

1 From the remaining outer border fabric, cut four 1³/4 in (4.5 cm) wide strips across the fabric width for the bindings.

2 Measure and sew the bindings to the sides first, then the top and bottom. Leave an extra 1 in (2.5 cm) extending at the ends of the top and bottom bindings for turning under at the corners.

3 Sew the bindings using a ³/8 in (1 cm) seam allowance, which gives a ³/8 in (1 cm) binding.

4 Attach a rod pocket to the back for hanging.

5 Make a label for your quilt, adding your name and the date and any other relevant details you wish.

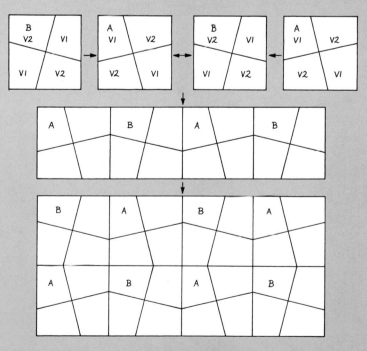

Quilt Layout Plan

Quilt Assembly Plan

The Hot Line

YOU WILL NEED

Note: Fabric quantities are calculated for 44 in (112 cm) wide fabric. The specified amounts are generous.

Purple gradation
- 6 in (15 cm) each of dark purple, medium-dark purple, medium purple fabric
- 4 in (10 cm) of light purple fabric

Yellow gradation
- 6 in (15 cm) each of mustard and medium yellow fabric
- 10 in (25 cm) of bright yellow fabric*
- 4 in (10 cm) of light yellow fabric

Burgundy/yellow gradation
- 8 in (20 cm) of burgundy fabric
- 6 in (15 cm) of red fabric
- 6 in (15 cm) of orange fabric
- an amount of bright yellow fabric which is included in the yellow gradation amounts
- 6 in (15 cm) of cream fabric for the unit centers
- 16 in (40 cm) of slate blue fabric for the units, borders and binding
- 24½ in (62 cm) square of fabric for the backing
- 24½ in (62 cm) square of batting

Continued on page 38

This small quilt is based on a 3 × 3 distorted grid. The design is symmetrical, so there are unit repeats. This is an excellent practice piece, before you tackle the other larger projects. Only two grid divisions need to be drafted and these will provide all the units needed to construct the quilt. Photocopy the layout plan and follow it carefully.

Finished size: 18½ in (46 cm) square

DRAFTING

See the Quilt Layout Plan on page 40.
Note: If you did the drafting exercises on pages 8–9, you will have already drafted the units and some of the logs. The design is symmetrical, so you only need the following units: B2, B3, C3, C4, A1, A2 and B1. When marking the foundations, these units are repeated. All the logs are drafted ⅜ in (1 cm) wide.

1 Draft the units onto graph paper, following the Quilt Layout Plan for measurements and the detailed instructions for "Drafting the Units" on pages 6–10. Refer to figures 1-8 for the number of logs to be drafted onto each unit.

2 Mark identification numbers in the centers of the units. Mark color placements onto the outside logs of the units.

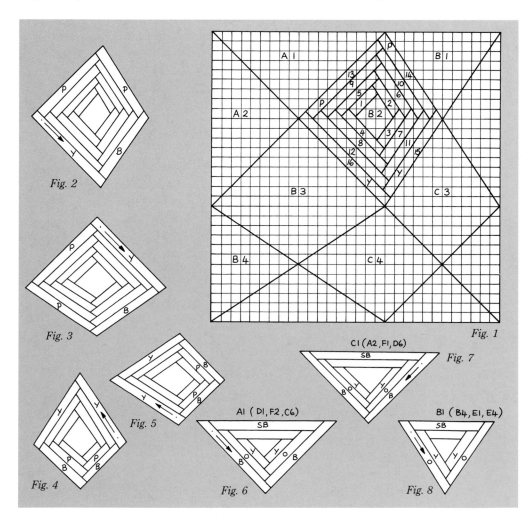

Fig. 2

Fig. 3

Fig. 5

Fig. 4

Fig. 6

Fig. 1

C1 (A2 ,F1 ,D6)
Fig. 7

A1 (D1, F2 ,C6)

B1 (B4, E1, E4)
Fig. 8

- basic sewing and drafting equipment
- one skein of embroidery floss for tying
- 24 in (60 cm) of medium-weight, non-fusible interfacing
- neutral-colored thread for the piecing
- navy thread for sewing the borders and binding

3 Turn the graph paper over and transfer all markings to this side. This is the side you will be marking from. There is no need to mark the direction arrows as the units are rotated into position.

MARKING THE FOUNDATIONS

Note: As this is a small project, mark all the foundations before piecing. Refer to the detailed instructions for "Preparing and Marking the Foundations" on pages 11–12.

For the inner units:

1 From the interfacing, cut two 6 in (15 cm) wide strips. Press, then cut them into twelve 6 in (15 cm) squares. These will be too big for some of the units; the excess is trimmed away after piecing.

2 The repeating units are as follows:
- B2 is the same as D2, E3 and C5, so mark it four times;
- B3 is the same as C2, E2, and D5, so mark it four times;
- C3 is the same as D4, so mark it twice; and
- C4 is the same as D3, so mark it twice.

There are twelve inner units. When marking the units, transfer all the identification marks and label each repeat with its correct name.

For the triangle units:

1 From the interfacing, cut two 4 in (10 cm) wide strips. Press. Refer to the detailed instructions for marking the "Edge and Corner Triangle Units" on page 12.

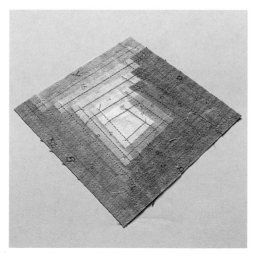

Sample 1: Unit B2 marked onto foundation.

Sample 2: Pieced unit C3.

Sample 3: Pieced unit B2.

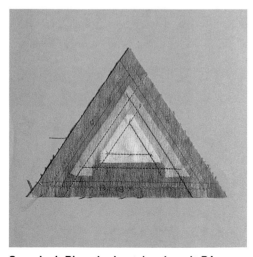

Sample 4: Pieced edge triangle unit B1.

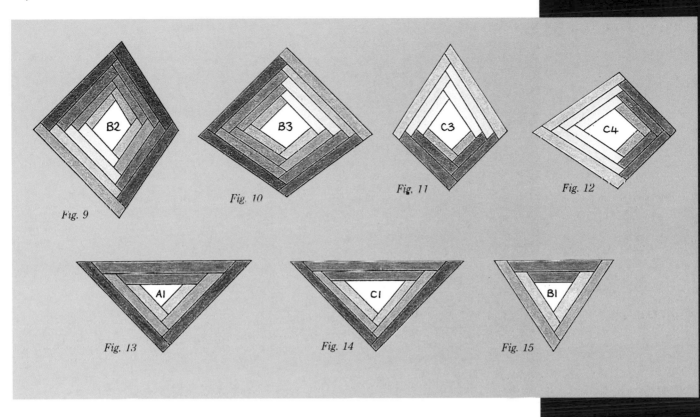

Fig. 9 — B2
Fig. 10 — B3
Fig. 11 — C3
Fig. 12 — C4
Fig. 13 — A1
Fig. 14 — C1
Fig. 15 — B1

2 The repeating units are as follows:
■ Corner triangle A1 is the same as D1, F2 and C6, so mark it four times;
■ Corner triangle C1 is the same as F1, D6 and A2, so mark it four times;
■ Edge triangle B1 is the same as B4, E1 and E4, so mark it four times.
There are twelve edge triangles. When marking the units, transfer all the identification marks and label each repeat with its correct name.

CUTTING THE FABRIC

Note: Cut the suggested number of strips to begin, then cut more as required.
1 From the cream fabric, cut two 1 1/2 in (5 cm) wide strips.
2 From the slate blue fabric, cut two 1 1/4 in (3 cm) wide strips. These are for the outside edges of the edge and corner triangles.
3 From each of the burgundy, red, orange and bright yellow fabrics, cut two 1 in (2.5 cm) wide strips.
4 From each of the mustard, bright yellow, medium yellow and light yellow fabrics, cut two 1 in (2.5 cm) wide strips.

5 From each of the dark purple, medium-dark purple, medium purple and light purple fabrics, cut two 1 in (2.5 cm) wide strips.
6 Cut snippets of all the selected fabrics and tape them in their gradated order on the photocopied layout plan. Refer to them when piecing, to keep the order correct.

PIECING THE UNITS

Note: For the center units C3, C4, D3 and D4, note that the yellow gradation uses the three lightest fabrics and the purple gradation uses the second and third fabrics. The outside log is burgundy.

1 Piece all the units, referring to the detailed instructions for "Foundation Piecing" on page 13, figures 9-15 and samples 1–4.
2 Stay-stitch around each unit, then trim the excess seam allowances to 3/8 in (1 cm).
3 After piecing a unit, pin it in place on the design wall. On the layout plan, draw a line with the fluorescent marker in the unit you have pieced to show that it is finished.

ASSEMBLY

Note: This quilt is joined together in four identical quarters. Study the Quilt Assembly Plan and refer to detailed instructions for Joining Units into Groups" and "Joining Groups to Form Rows or Sections" on pages 16–17. Use plenty of pins, matching dots and sewing lines. All seam lines are straight and sewn from edge to edge. Press the seam allowances open.

Study the layout plan to make sure the repeat units are in their correct places. Assemble the four quarters, join them into halves, then join the two halves to form the quilt top. Press all the seams open.

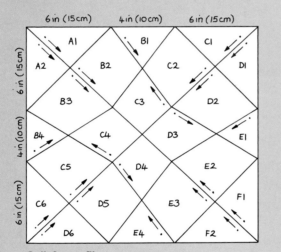

Quilt Layout Plan

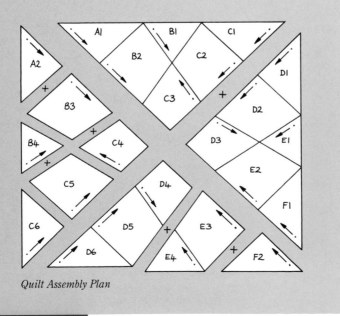

Quilt Assembly Plan

BORDERS

Note: If the units have been properly trimmed, there should be a $3/8$ in (1 cm) seam allowance extending beyond the outside marked lines on the units. Refer to the detailed instructions for "Borders" on pages 18–19.

1   From the border fabric, cut two $2^{1}/4$ in (6 cm) wide strips across the fabric width. Cut them in half to get four $2^{1}/4$ in (6 cm) wide strips.

2   Attach the borders, using a $3/8$ in (1 cm) seam; attach the side borders first, then the top and bottom borders.

LAYERING

Refer to the detailed instructions for "Layering" on page 20.
Assemble the three layers of the quilt. Pin-baste the layers together.

TYING AND QUILTING

Refer to the detailed instructions for "Tying" and "Machine-quilting" on pages 20–21.

1   On the back, tie the quilt at all the major seam intersections using the embroidery floss. The seam junctions can be felt through the backing.

2   Machine-quilt in the ditch around the border.

FINISHING

Refer to the detailed instructions for "Binding", "Rod Pocket", and Labeling Your Quilt" on page 21.

1   Trim the edges of the quilt layers, leaving a $1^{1}/4$ in (3 cm) wide border. Baste or pin baste around the cut edges.

2   Cut two $1^{3}/4$ in (4.5 cm) wide strips the width of the fabric. Cut them in half to yield four $1^{3}/4$ in (4.5 cm) wide strips.

3   Measure and apply the binding as for the borders, using a $3/8$ in (1 cm) seam. Sew the sides first, then the top and bottom. Leave 1 in (2.5 cm) extending on the top and bottom strips to allow for turning under.

4   Attach a rod pocket or hanging loops to the back, then a label.

Green Frames

The grid for this small quilt is not very complicated, but take care when drafting. Some of the units have a wide/narrow log variation and others have an even and uneven variation. The quilt is joined in four identical quarters, so only one quarter needs to be drafted.

Finished size: 27 in (68.5 cm) square

UNIT DRAFTING

See the Quilt Layout Plan on page 45.

1 Photocopy the layout plan.
2 Referring to "The Grid" on page 6 and the Quilt Layout Plan, draft one only of Units A, B, Br, C, D, Dr and E; edge and corner triangles F and G.

DRAFTING THE LOGS

Note: Refer to the detailed instructions for "Drafting the Units" on pages 6–10 and the unit drafting diagrams (below). All the measurements for the log widths are given. Do not alter them.

There are two variations of logs in this project: even and uneven. Refer to figures 1 to 9 (below) showing the drafted logs. The even log widths vary; wide are 1/2 in (12 mm), and 3/8 in (1 cm) and narrow are 5/16 in (8 mm) wide.

The uneven logs are marked with the narrow ends 1/4 in (6 mm) wide and the wide ends at 1/2 in (12 mm) wide.

YOU WILL NEED

Note: Fabric quantities are calculated for 44 in (112 cm) wide fabric. The specified amounts are generous. The fabrics are all solids in gradations from light to dark.

For the green gradation:
- 24 in (60 cm) of dark green fabric (includes borders and bindings) (Dg)
- 8 in (20 cm) of medium dark green fabric (Mdg)
- 8 in (20 cm) of medium green fabric (Mg)
- 8 in (20 cm) of medium light green fabric (Mlg)
- 4 in (10 cm) of light green fabric (Lg)

For the red gradation:
- 4 in (10 cm) of dark plum fabric (Dp)
- 4 in (10 cm) of burgundy fabric (B)
- 6 in (15 cm) of red fabric (R)
- 4 in (10 cm) of dull orange fabric (Do)
- an amount of mustard fabric (M) which is included in the yellow run

For the yellow gradation:
- 8 in (20 cm) of mustard fabric (M)
- 8 in (20 cm) of medium yellow fabric (My)
- 10 in (26 cm) of medium light yellow fabric (Mly)
- 8 in (20 cm) of light yellow fabric (Ly)

Continued on page 42

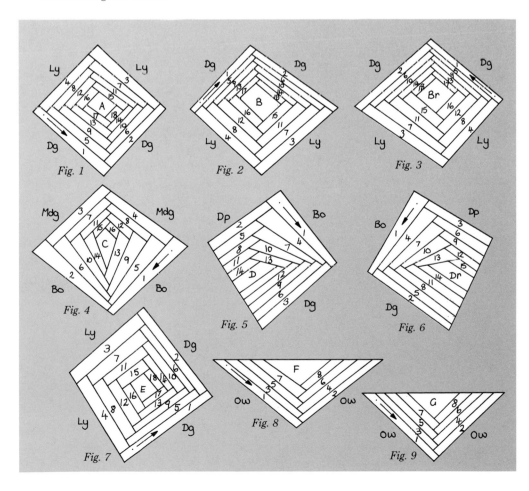

Fig. 1
Fig. 2
Fig. 3
Fig. 4
Fig. 5
Fig. 6
Fig. 7
Fig. 8
Fig. 9

- 4 in (10 cm) of bright orange fabric (Bo)
- 8 in (20 cm) of off-white fabric (Ow)
- 34 in (86 cm) of fabric for the backing
- 34 in (86 cm) of 48 in (122 cm) wide Pellon batting
- 1.6 m (2 yd) of interfacing
- basic sewing and drafting equipment
- dark green thread for joining the units and rows, borders and binding neutral-colored thread for piecing
- embroidery floss to match or contrast with the backing fabric

For Unit A (Fig. 1):

The logs are all even and narrow $5/16$ in (8 mm) wide. The unit has five logs on two sides and four logs on the other two sides of the center. To draft, follow the direction arrow and draft four logs on either side of the center, then add two more. Mark sixteen foundations.

Fabrics used – All sixteen units have red centers. The two sides that have five logs are pieced using the green gradation, beginning with light green and ending with dark green. The remaining two sides which have four logs are pieced using the yellow gradation, beginning with mustard and ending with light yellow (Fig. 10).

For Units B and B reversed (Br) (Figs 2 and 3):

These use a combination of even logs, wide $3/8$ in (1 cm) and narrow $5/16$ in (8 mm). The units have five narrow logs on two sides of the center and four wide logs on the remaining two sides. The drafting begins with two narrow logs, then two wide logs. Repeat until there are four on either side of the center, then draft another two narrow logs. Note that the logs in Unit B spiral in a clockwise direction and the logs in Unit Br spiral in a counter-clockwise direction. Mark four B and four Br foundations.

Fabrics used – All units have red centers. All the narrow logs are pieced using the five fabric green gradation, beginning with light green and ending with dark green. The wide logs are pieced using the four fabric yellow gradation, beginning with mustard and ending with light yellow (Figs 11 and 12).

For Unit C (Fig. 4):

This unit has a combination of logs, even and uneven. The even logs are narrow $5/16$ in (8 mm); the uneven logs are $1/2$ in (12 mm) at the wide end tapering to $1/4$ in (6 mm) at the narrow end. There are four logs on either side of the center. Mark four.

Fabrics used – All units have red centers. The even logs are pieced in the green gradation, beginning with light green and ending with medium dark green. The uneven logs are pieced in the yellow gradation in the following order: light yellow, medium, mustard and bright orange (Fig. 13).

For Units D and D reversed (Dr) (Figs 5 and 6):

These have a combination of even and uneven logs. The even logs are narrow $5/16$ in (8 mm); the uneven logs are $1/2$ in (12 mm) at the wide end tapering to $1/4$ in (6 mm) at the narrow end. Five logs are drafted on only three sides around the center shape. Mark four D and four Dr. Pay careful attention to the drafting diagrams.

Fabrics used – All centers are off-white. The uneven logs are pieced in the yellow gradation which is different for D and Dr. For Unit D, begin with light yellow and end with mustard. The last outside uneven log (the fifth) is dull orange (Fig. 14). For Unit Dr, use the yellow color gradation also, but finish with bright orange for the outside log, instead of dull orange (Fig. 15).

The even logs for both Units D and Dr are pieced using the red gradation, beginning with mustard and ending with dark plum. The other side is pieced using the green gradation, beginning with light green and ending with dark green.

For Unit E (Fig. 7):

This has a combination of even logs, wide $1/2$ in (12 mm) and narrow $5/16$ in (8 mm). Draft in the same way as Unit Br, with logs spiraling counter-clockwise. Mark four times.

Fabrics used – All the units have red centers and the color placement is identical to Unit A (Fig. 16).

For edge triangle Unit F (Fig. 8):

This has even, narrow logs which are $5/16$ in (8 mm). Draft four logs on the two short sides of the triangle. Mark four times.

Fabrics used – The centers are all dark green. The even logs are pieced using the yellow gradation, beginning with mustard through to medium yellow, medium light yellow and ending with off-white, instead of pale yellow (Fig. 17).

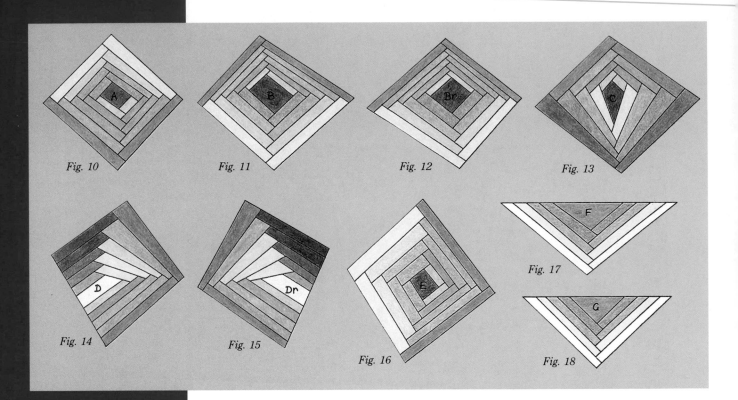

Fig. 10   Fig. 11   Fig. 12   Fig. 13

Fig. 14   Fig. 15   Fig. 16   Fig. 17

Fig. 18

For edge triangle and corner triangles Unit G (Fig. 9):

These are drafted in the same way as Unit F. The color placement is also identical (Fig. 18). Mark sixteen times.

MARKING THE FOUNDATIONS

Note: Refer to the detailed instructions for "Preparing and Marking the Foundation" on pages 11–12.

1 Cut the interfacing into seven 6 in (15 cm) wide strips, then cut them into forty 6 in (15 cm) squares. These are for the inner units. Cut the edge triangle strips later.

2 When marking the foundations, I suggest you also mark the fabric placement. Colors are indicated in figures 10-18 and in the materials list.

CUTTING THE FABRIC

1 Cut one 1¹/4 in (3 cm) wide strip from both orange fabrics. Cut a 1 in (2.5 cm) wide strip from the remaining fabrics. Cut more as required.

2 Cut a 2 in (5 cm) wide red strip for the unit centers.

3 Cut a 2 in (5 cm) wide dark green strip for the centers of Units F and G.

4 Cut a 2 in (5 cm) wide off-white strip for the centers for Units D and Dr.

PIECING THE UNITS

Note: Refer to the detailed instructions for Foundation Piecing on page 13.

Because of the reversals and repeats with this design, it is better to begin piecing with the center units (E) and work toward the outside, piecing the triangle units last. Follow the fabric piecing order carefully.

For the corner and edge triangles:

1 Cut four 4 in (10 cm) wide strips of interfacing. Lay a strip over triangle F, leaving a ¹/2 in (12 mm) seam allowance extending beyond the marked lines. Mark the foundation. Make sure you extend the sewing lines out through the outside marked line. Cut the marked triangle from the strip. Check to make sure there is adequate seam allowance extending around it. Repeat for the remaining four F triangles.

2 Repeat for triangle G, marking sixteen of them.

JOINING THE UNITS

Note: Refer to the detailed instructions for "Joining Units into Groups" on page 15.

Check to make sure the units are in their right positions on the design wall. You cannot rely on direction arrows as the units repeat and are rotated into position.

The quilt is assembled in four quarters. Follow the piecing order as shown in figures 19 and 20. You will need to release seam allowances to join the rows to form the quarters. These are indicated on the diagrams with a small arrow.

When joining the quarters together, all seams are straight (Fig. 21). Sew with all of the seam allowances open. Press all the seams open.

BORDERS

Note: Refer to the detailed instructions for "Borders" on pages 18–19.

Cut four 2¹/₂ in (6.5 cm) wide strips across the width of the dark green fabric. Measure and sew the borders, joining them to the sides first, then to the top and bottom. Press the seams towards the borders.

TYING

Note: Refer to the detailed instructions for "Tying" on pages 20–21.

Assemble the layers, ready for tying. Tie the quilt on the back first, then run a row of machine-stitching in the border ditch. Trim the excess layers to have a finished border width of 1¹/₂ in (4 cm).

FINISHING

Note: Refer to the detailed instructions for "Binding", "Rod Pocket", and "Labeling Your Quilt" on page 21.

1 Cut four 1³/4 in (4.5 cm) wide strips across the width of the dark green fabric. Measure and attach the binding in the same way as for the borders. Leave an extra 1 in (2.5 cm) extending at both ends of the top and bottom binding strips for turning at the corners. The finished binding width will be ³/8 in (1 cm).

2 Attach a rod pocket on the back for hanging, and label your quilt.

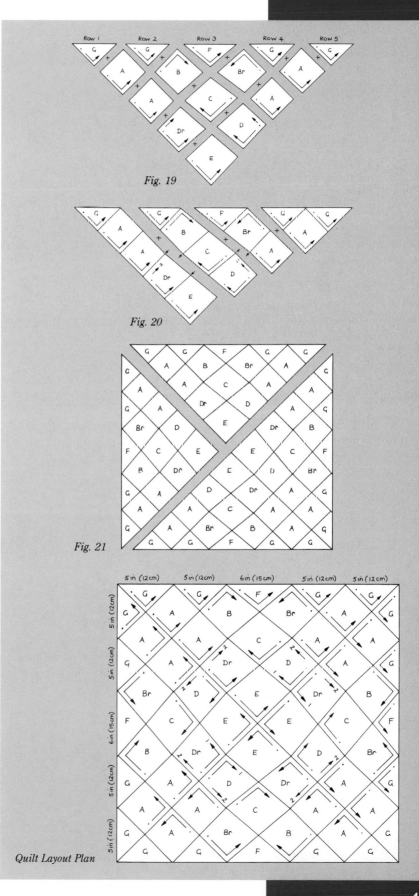

Fig. 19

Fig. 20

Fig. 21

Quilt Layout Plan

Colors 2

YOU WILL NEED

NOTE: You will need a wide range of fabrics in gradated shades in all color families. The wider the range, the more varied your choices will be. Fabric quantities are calculated for 44 in (112 cm) wide fabric. The specified amounts are generous.

- **4 in (10 cm) each of an assortment of solid fabrics in thirty to forty different colors, in as wide a range as possible**
- **8 in (20 cm) each of five or six assorted dark fabrics for the outer units**
- **16 in (40 cm) of navy fabric for the borders and binding**
- **2¹/2 yd (2 m) of medium-weight interfacing**
- **1¹/8 yd (1 m) of fabric for the backing**
- **1¹/8 yd (1 m) of Pellon batting**
- **basic sewing and drafting equipment**
- **neutral-colored thread for the piecing**
- **medium grey thread for joining the units**
- **matching thread for the binding**
- **one skein of embroidery floss for tying**

After completing some of the projects for this book, I found myself knee-deep in leftover scraps. In an effort to use them up, I decided I would make a quilt similar to my quilt 'From a Distance' that is in the Colors of Australia touring exhibition. Hence the name 'Colors 2'. Needless to say, after completing the quilt, I ended up with double the number of leftover strips!

Finished size: 32¹/2 in (78 cm) square

DRAFTING

See the Quilt Layout Plan on page 51.
Note: Refer to the detailed instructions for "Drafting the Units" on pages 6–10. This small quilt is composed of uneven spiraling logs. Logs are drafted onto every unit in the same clockwise direction. Every log begins narrow and ends wide. When drafting the first round of logs (the four longest outside ones), make sure that the narrow end is ³/16 in (5 mm) or wider. If it is any narrower than this, you will not be able to trim the seam allowances down enough so the outside marked lines are visible. The resulting seam allowance will be very narrow. If you don't, then the unit joining seams will not lie flat when pressed open (see Sample 1). The wide ends of the logs should never be any wider than ¹/2 in (12 mm). The remaining logs in the units are pieced at random widths, still having wide and narrow ends. Draw in the lines for the first two units in pencil to get used to ruling uneven logs. When you are satisfied, draw over them with the felt-tipped pen.

1 Photocopy the quilt layout plan.
2 As this quilt is better constructed beginning in the middle, start by drafting the inner Units (F6, F7 and G6, G7). The grid to rule up for these units is shown

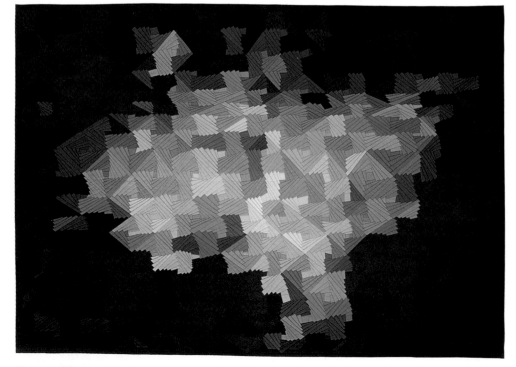

From a Distance.

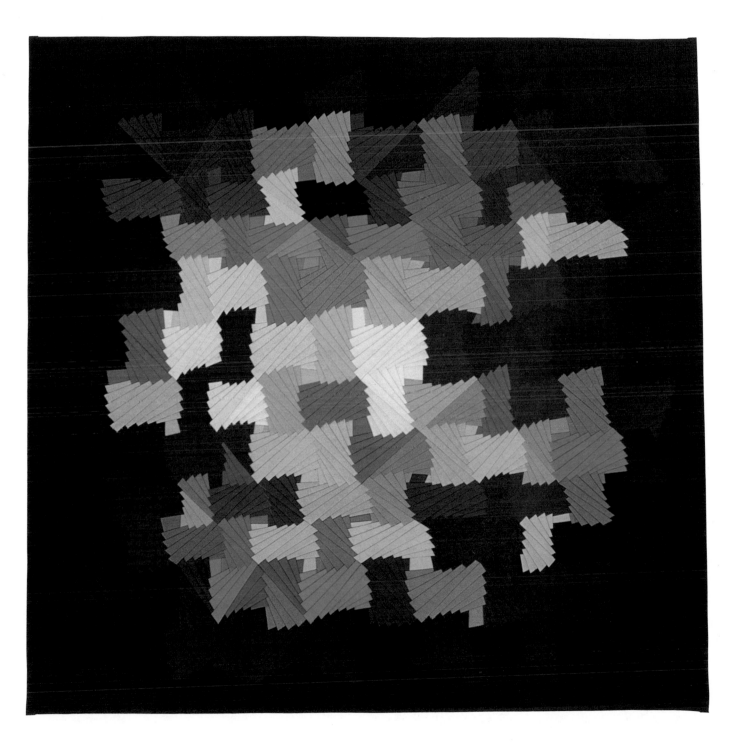

on the Quilt Layout Plan. If you have trouble locating the grid, lightly rule the vertical and horizontal grid on the photocopied plan.

The number of logs on either side of the center shape can vary, depending upon the size of the unit. Some will have four logs on either side and others will have five. Some will have four on two sides and five on the other two sides. Some of the larger units will need six logs around the center shape. If the center shape looks too big, add another log or two. If it looks too small, eliminate some logs. There is no specific number of logs required for the units.

3 Label every unit after drafting the logs and make sure you mark the directional arrow at the top (Fig. 1). Turn the drafted units over and transfer all markings to the back of the graph paper (Fig. 2). This is essential for this quilt.

For the edge triangles:
The edge triangles are repeated. They are drafted with three uneven logs on either side of the resulting central triangular shape with the logs all spiraling in the same direction. There is no need to draft logs onto every one. You only need to draft logs onto one triangle from each group.

Goup 1
Draft Unit B1 and mark it eight times for units B1, B4, E1, E10, H1, H10, L1, and L4, labeling each with these identifying numbers.

Group 2
Draft Unit C1 and mark it four times for units C1, C6, J1, and J8, labeling each with these identifying numbers.

Group 3
Draft Unit D1 and mark it four times for units D1, D8, K1, and K6, labeling each with these identifying numbers.

For the corner triangles:
The corner triangles, A1, A2, F1, G1, F12, G12, M1, and M2, are all the same size and the logs are drafted in the same way for all of them. Draft the logs onto one triangle, A1, then mark eight identical foundations from this.

MARKING THE FOUNDATIONS
Note: Refer to the detailed instructions for "Preparing and Marking the Foundation" on pages 11–12.

For the inner units:
1 Cut ten 6 in (15 cm) wide strips of interfacing. Cut them into sixty 6 in (15 cm) squares. You will need to cut six foundation squares from each strip.

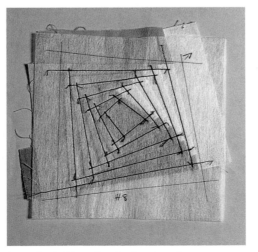

Sample 1: Pieced unit showing the narrow seam allowance left on all outside logs so that the outside marked line is visible.

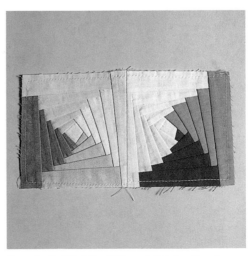

Sample 2: Slightly different fabrics flowing from one unit to another.

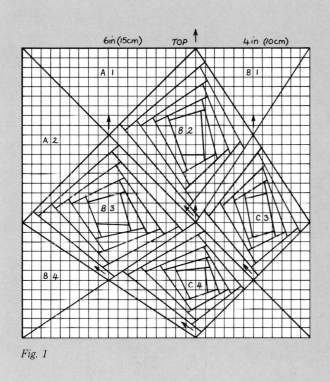

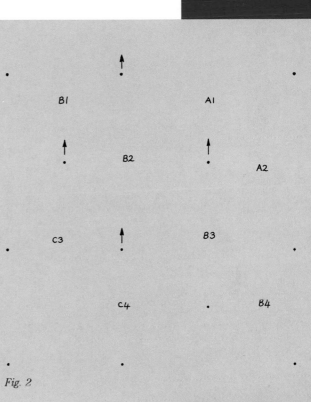

Fig. 1

Fig. 2

Some of these squares will be bigger than you need; you can trim the excess away later.

2 Begin to mark the foundations. Only mark a few groups at a time, beginning in the middle of the grid. Make sure you transfer all identification marks and especially the directional arrows.

For the triangle units:
Cut four 4 in (10 cm) wide strips of interfacing. Mark the triangles onto the foundation. Mark an * in the seam allowance at the outside edge of each one. Make sure you mark each one with the correct identification number.

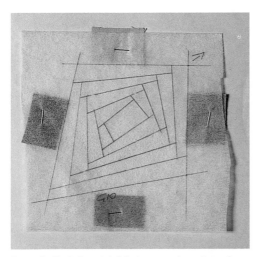

Sample 3: Selected fabric samples pinned onto the unmarked (right) side of the foundation for fabric placement.

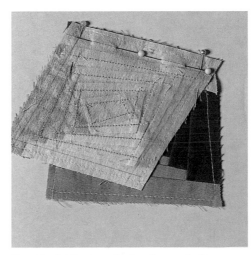

Sample 4: Pin-matched units ready for sewing.

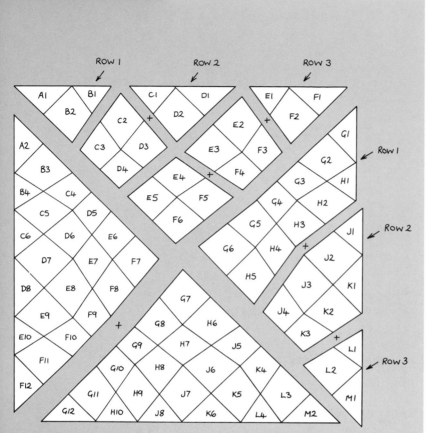

Fig. 3

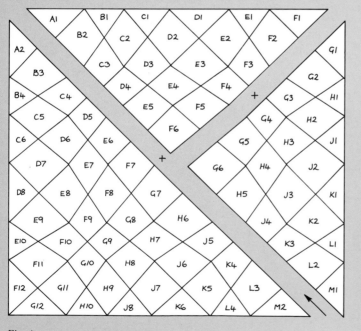

Fig. 4

CUTTING THE FABRIC

From each of the assorted solid fabrics, cut two 1¼ in (3 cm) wide strips.

Note: There is no color placement plan for this quilt. You can follow the picture of my quilt or design your own version. Pin the marked units onto the design wall with the right side (unmarked) facing out. Cut pieces, approximately 1 in x 1½ in (2.5 cm x 5 cm) from selected fabrics and pin them to the units on the design wall so you can audition them. The centers can be any one of the four selected fabrics. The colors flow from one unit to the next. They can be the same fabric or slightly different (see sample 2).

Don't be afraid to put together fabrics you normally wouldn't place side by side. I find it easier to work with three or four units at one time. When you are satisfied with your color placement, pin the small pieces in place onto the unmarked side of the units. This is your color placement plan for piecing (see Sample 3).

PIECING THE UNITS

Note: Refer to the detailed instructions for "Foundation Piecing" on page 13.

1 Piece the units one at a time. Remove the small pieces of fabric after the first round of logs has been sewn in place.

2 After making the first group of units, plan and piece the units of another section. Don't try to plan your color placement too far ahead. You do however need to have an idea of what areas are to be light, medium and dark. The outside units are all dark and the fabrics from these flow into the edge triangles.

3 Piece all the units, corner and edge triangles. Do not attempt to join them up until they are all pieced.

ASSEMBLY

Note: The quilt is assembled in four quarters (Fig. 3). Press all the seams open. As some seam allowances must be released, make sure you backstitch at the corner dots. Pin-match all the corner dots, along the marked sewing lines and any seam allowance junctions (see Sample 4).

1. Join the inside units to form three groups of four units. There are three of these groups in each quarter, as shown in the top quarter of figure 3. You will have to release some of the seams so the group will lay flat.
2. Join two edge triangles and one inside unit into groups of three as shown (A1, B1, B2). There are three of these groups in each quarter. These can all be sewn edge to edge.
3. After assembling the groups, join them together into rows.
4. Assemble the four quarters, then join them two by two into halves as shown in figure 4. This seam is not straight.
5. Join the two halves together to form the quilt top. Note that this last seam is straight. You can sew straight through from edge to edge.
6. Press well. If you trimmed every unit after piecing, there should be a 3/8 in (1 cm) seam allowance around the outside edges. If not, trim them now.

BORDERS

Note: Refer to the detailed instructions for "Borders" on pages 18–19.
1. From the navy fabric cut four 2 in (5 cm) wide strips, cutting across the grain. These will be too big, trim them later.
2. Mark a 3/8 in (1 cm) seam allowance along one long side of each strip.
3. Attach the borders to the sides first, then to the top and bottom. Press the seams towards the borders.

LAYERING

Note: Refer to the detailed instructions for "Layering" on page 20.
Assemble the quilt layers. Use plenty of pins to hold the layers together. Pin in the center of every second unit, and along the edges of the quilt center next to the borders and again at the outer edges. Begin in the center and work outward.

TYING AND QUILTING

Note: Refer to the detailed instructions for "Tying" and "Machine-quilting" on pages 20–21.

1. Turn the quilt over and tie every second seam junction, beginning at the center and working outward.
2. Turn the quilt over again and thread-baste in the border just beyond the seam allowance and 1/2 in (12 mm) in from the edges. Remove all the pins.
3. Machine quilt in the border ditch.
4. Trim the excess batting and backing, leaving a 1 3/8 in (3.5 cm) border. This leaves a 1 in (2.5 cm) wide narrow border after binding.

FINISHING

Note: Refer to the detailed instructions for "Binding", "Rod Pocket", and "Labeling Your Quilt" on page 21.
1. From the binding fabric, cut four 1 3/4 in (4.5 cm) wide strips across the width of the fabric.
2. Measure and sew the binding in place. Bind the sides first, then the top and bottom.
3. Add a rod pocket to the back for hanging, and label your quilt.

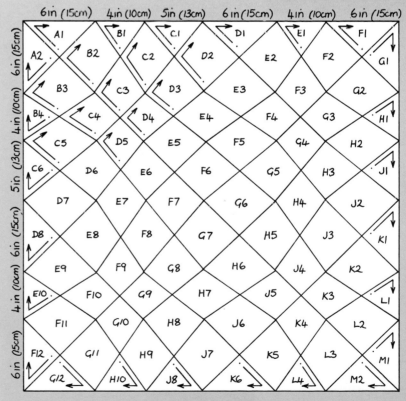

6in (15cm) 4in (10cm) 5in (13cm) 6in (15cm) 4in (10cm) 6in (15cm)

Quilt Layout Plan

Fanciful

YOU WILL NEED

Note: Fabric requirements are calculated for 44 in (112 cm) wide fabric. The given amounts are generous.

- 12 in (30 cm) each of dark and medium/dark green fabric
- 10 in (25 cm) each of medium and light green fabric
- 2¹/2 in (6 cm) of each of four fabrics from dark to light to form a set for the fan effect (blues, reds, yellows, purples, oranges and pinks)

Continued on page 54

This small quilt uses color gradations and runs from many color families to form bright fans that march diagonally across the surface. The fans are formed by the specific placement of the uneven logs. Some of the fabric gradations are repeated more than once in the quilt.

It is a great project for using up leftover strips from other quilts. Sort your strips into pleasing groups of four, going from dark to light. The green gradation is consistent throughout the quilt. The dark areas are a combination of black, dark and medium-dark blues and dark purples. This mix introduces relief to the dark areas.

The quilt has a multiple border, using a multi-striped fabric to highlight the inner fabrics and to act as a frame. There is a meandering pattern machine-quilted in the border areas. The pieced area has been tied.

Finished size: 36¹/2 in (93 cm) square

DRAFTING

See the Quilt Layout Plan below.

Note: Refer to the detailed instructions for "Drafting the Units" on pages 6–10.

1 Photocopy the Quilt Layout Plan.
2 The units are drafted with a combination of even and uneven logs. The first log in every unit is uneven and begins wide. The second log is also uneven and begins narrow (Fig. 1). Even logs are all ⁵/16 in (8 mm) wide and are all dark.

Draft the units, referring to the Quilt Layout Plan. Label each unit with its name and include the direction arrow at the top. Mark the log direction arrows onto the drafted units in their correct positions.

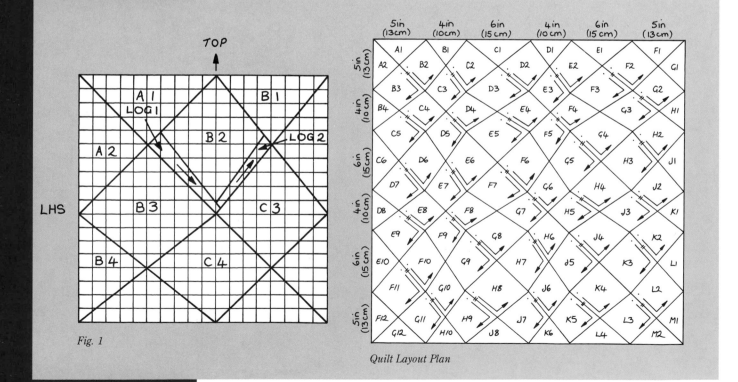

Fig. 1

Quilt Layout Plan

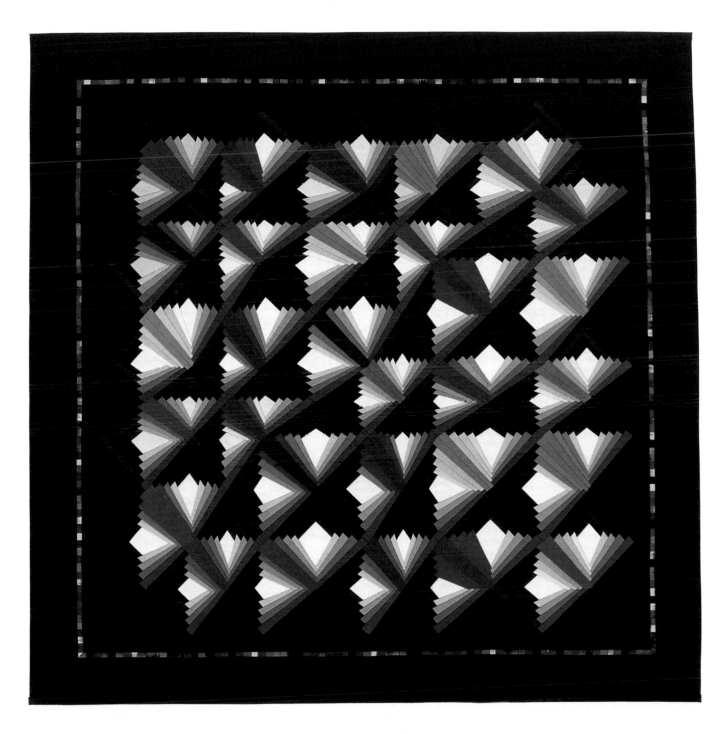

- 10 in (25 cm) each of white and cream fabric for the unit centers (I have used a few very pale blues and pinks in the centers of some of the top units)
- 40 in (102 cm) total of dark fabric (black, dark blue, medium dark blue, dark purple)
- 1 2/3 yd (1.5 m) of black fabric for the edge triangles, inner and outer borders and binding
- 6 in (15 cm) of multi-striped fabric
- basic sewing and drafting equipment
- 2 1/4 yd (2.1 m) of medium-weight interfacing
- one skein of embroidery floss to match the backing fabric
- neutral-colored thread for piecing
- medium/dark grey thread for joining units and rows
- 40 in (112 cm) of fabric for the backing
- 40 in (112 cm) of Pellon batting

For the uneven logs:

1 All the narrow ends of the longest outside logs are 1/4 in (6 mm) wide, with the wide ends at 1/2 in (12 mm) wide. Draft the remaining uneven logs, beginning and ending with widths of your choice, making sure the wide ends do not exceed 1/2 in (12 mm).

    When drafting the uneven logs, the size of the unit will dictate the width of the logs. The bigger the unit, the wider the logs (see Unit E5). Small units have narrower logs (see Unit D4). All units have four logs on either side of the center (Fig. 2).

    I recommend that you draft the logs onto the first group of units using a pencil to see how wide or narrow you need to draft the logs to make them fit. Adjust widths, if necessary, then draw over them with the black pen.

2 The fans go diagonally across the quilt (Fig. 3). The green fabric run is at the bottom edge of the fan units. After drafting the logs, indicate the placement for the green fabric in the uneven logs on the bottom diagonal edge of the units (Fig. 2). The other uneven logs in the units are for the color runs that form the fans.

3 Turn the graph paper over and transfer all the marks to this side. The direction arrows and green placement are the most important. You can mark all the units now or do them as required.

MARKING THE FOUNDATIONS
Note: The inner units are marked first. The edge triangles will be marked later. Refer to the detailed instructions for "Preparing and Marking the Foundation" on pages 11–12.

For the inner units:

1 Cut ten 5 1/2 in (14.5 cm) wide strips of interfacing. Press them to pre-shrink. Layer them together, then cut them into sixty 5 1/2 in (14.5 cm) squares. These will be way too big for some of the units. Trim the excess away after the unit has been pieced and stay-stitched.

2 Mark the foundations. Pin the two foundations that form a fan, for example B2 and B3, together; they will be pieced at the same time as they use the same fabrics. The fan units are indicated by a symbol (=) marked across the common seam on the "Quilt Layout Plan". They can also be identified by the direction of the arrows. When the arrows lie together in adjacent units, it indicates a fan unit.

Sample 1: Fabric mock-ups stitched onto interfacing to help with color placement.

Sample 2: Seam allowance trimmed so the outside marked lines are visible.

CUTTING THE FABRIC

To audition the fabrics for the fan sections, make fabric mock-ups of intended fabric groupings. I sewed my selections onto scraps of interfacing, as I knew I wanted to repeat some of them (see Sample 1).

1 For the cream or white unit centers, cut two 1¼ in (3 in) wide strips; cut more as needed.

2 For the green gradation, cut four strips of the darkest fabric, 1¼ in (3 cm) wide. Cut four strips each of the other three fabrics 1 in (2.5 cm) wide. Cut more strips as required.

3 For the gradations and runs, cut one 1¼ in (3 cm) wide strip from all four fabrics in the grouping.

4 For the dark blue/black/purple fabrics, cut four 1 in (2.5 cm) wide strips from each. Cut more strips as required.

FOUNDATION PIECING

Note: Refer to the detailed instructions for "Foundation Piecing" on page 13.

For the unit centers:

Lay the foundation over the cream strip, marked side facing up. Cut away the excess, leaving plenty of seam allowance extending around the central shape. This is called 'rough cutting'.

For the inner units:

Note: When piecing the uneven logs, be careful not to sew over the next marked line at the narrow ends. This is easily done because there is not much room. If necessary, stop stitching and backstitch right at the end of the line you are sewing on. On the two outside uneven logs, the seam allowances must be trimmed close to the stitching so you can see the outside marked line clearly (see Sample 2).

The green and gradated fabrics begin with the lightest log and end with the darkest log. The dark fabrics are selected randomly (see Sample 3).

1 Piece two matched fan units at the same time, for example, B2 and B3, D4 and D5. After stay-stitching and trimming the units, pin them in place on your design

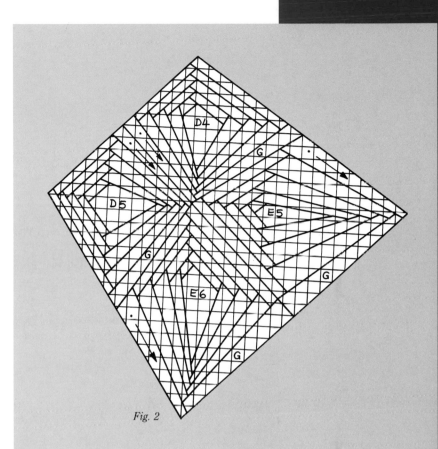

Fig. 2

Fig. 3

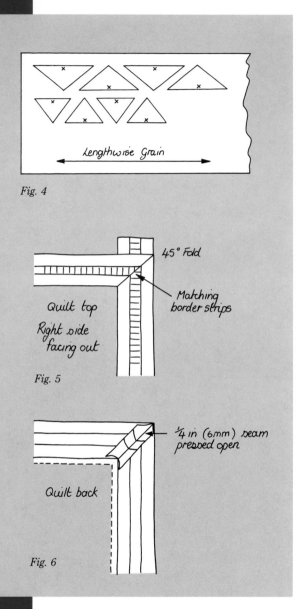

Fig. 4

Fig. 5

Fig. 6

Sample 3: Pieced unit showing fabric placement.

wall. Do not sew the fan units together as the quilt is assembled in four sections.

2 Piece all the inner fan units.

MARKING AND PIECING THE EDGE TRIANGLES

1 Cut five 4 in (10 cm) wide strips of interfacing. Press to pre-shrink them.

2 There are three repeat groups, totalling twenty-four edge triangles.

Group 1
A1, A2, F1, G1, F12, G12, M1, M2

Group 2
C1, C6, E1, E10, J1, J8, L1, L4

Group 3
B1, B4, D1, D8, H1, H10, K1, K6

Mark triangles A1, C1, and B1 eight times each. Label each repeat with its correct number from the appropriate group above. To mark, lay the interfacing strip over A1, making sure there is plenty of space beyond all the outside marked lines of the triangle for the seam allowance. Tape it lightly in place. Mark the three corner dots, then mark the lines, extending the lines right through all corner dots. Put an * in the seam allowance at the long outside edge. Release the tape and cut the marked triangle from the strip. Lay the strip over the triangle again and repeat. Label each triangle with its correct placement number. Repeat for all the groups.

Cutting

1 From the black fabric, cut a 28 in (70 cm) long section. This is for the borders and binding. Set it aside.

2 Lay the remaining black fabric, in single thickness, onto a flat surface, right side facing down. Make sure it is pressed well with no creases. Place the edge triangle foundations onto it, marked sides facing up. Have the edge with the marked cross running on the lengthwise grain. Nest them, leaving enough room between them to cut them apart (Fig. 4).

3 Pin the foundations to the fabric and cut them apart. To make the foundation stick to the black fabric, press the two together, then stay-stitch around the three sides just outside the marked line.

4 Using the rotary cutter and ruler, trim all the edges down to 3/8 in (1 cm). This is important because the bindings will be sewn directly to the long edges of the triangles.

5 Place the triangles into their correct positions around the edges of the inner units. The edges marked with a cross are the outside edges of the quilt.

ASSEMBLY

Note: The quilt is constructed in four sections as shown in the Quilt Assembly Plan on page 58. Within each section some units are joined into groups of four, others into groups of two. All four sections have edge triangle units. These are all indicated on the assembly plan with heavy black lines. The corner triangles (F1,G1,F12 and G12) are sewn together to form triangle units. The other corner triangles are sewn individually to adjoining units. You will have to release the center seam allowance when joining many of the groups of four. Make sure you sew from edge to edge and backstitch every seam at the corner dots. Throughout the whole joining process, pin-match the corner dots and use lots of pins to match the sewing lines. If a joining seam will not sit flat, just release the stitches in the seam allowance as far as the corner dot. Press all the seams open.

1 Join the groups into rows, then join the rows together to form the four sections. Join two sections together, twice, to form two halves.

2 Join the two halves to complete the quilt top. The last seam sewn to form the quilt top is sewn from the top left-hand corner to the bottom right-hand corner. This last seam is straight. All seam allowances which you sew across should be pressed open.

BORDERS

Note: Refer to the detailed instructions for "Borders" on pages 18–19.

The borders are comprised of two black and one multi-striped print. They are assembled as border units first, before being sewn to the quilt. The corners are mitered. Cut all strips across the fabric width. The strips are all cut too wide; the excess width is trimmed after they are sewn together. This gives a nice straight edge for attaching the border units to the quilt. Use 1/4 in (6 mm) seams for joining the strips together.

1 Using the section of black fabric put aside, cut the following strips across the fabric width:
- four 1 3/4 in (4.5 cm) wide strips for the inner border;
- four 3 in (7.5 cm) wide strips for the outer border.

2 From the multi-striped fabric, cut four 1 in (2.5 cm) wide strips.

3 Join a black inner border strip to a multi-striped strip. Press the seam towards the black strip.

4 Using the rotary cutter and ruler, trim the strips down to the following measurements: 1 3/8 in (3.5 cm) for the inner border and 1/2 in (12 mm) for the striped fabric.

5 Sew a black outer border strip to a multi-striped border strip. Press the seam towards the black strip. Repeat for all the border strip units. This results in a narrow 1/4 in (6 mm) strip of striped fabric. Any wider than this would be overpowering.

6 Mark a 3/8 in (1 cm) seam along the long edge of the inner border strips. Pin-mark the center on all four edges of the quilt. Pin mark the center of all four border units in the inner border. Measure the quilt vertically and horizontally from outside the marked sewing lines. Mark this measurement onto the inner border strips, with half on either side of the center mark.

7 Matching the end pins on the borders with the corner marked dots and marked sewing lines, sew the borders to the quilt. Stop and start at the corner dots. Make sure you backstitch. Press the seams towards the borders.

8 To miter the corners, lay one corner on

the ironing board. Press the two border strips as flat and straight as possible. Fold under one border at an angle of 45 degrees (Fig. 5). Use the 45-degree line on the ruler to check that the angle is correct and that the striped borders meet. Adjust if necessary. Press the fold. Place a pin inside the pressed fold near the outside edge. Fold the quilt so that the borders are right sides together. Machine-baste along the pressed fold. Open it out to make sure the corner lies flat. If it does, re-sew with a normal stitch. Repeat for all four corners. Trim the excess away leaving a $1/4$ in (6 mm) seam allowance and press it open (Fig. 6).

LAYERING

Note: Refer to the detailed instructions for "Layering" on page 20.

Layer the backing, batting, and quilt top together on a flat surface. Beginning in the center, pin-baste in the center of every second unit and around the edges. Pin-baste along the inner border seam, in the narrow second border and around the edges of the outer border.

TYING AND QUILTING

Note: Refer to the detailed instructions for "Tying" and "Machine-quilting" on pages 20–21

1 Turn the quilt over and, beginning in the center, tie every second seam allowance join. You should be able to feel them. Turn the quilt over and remove the pins from the inner pieced section. Leave the other pins in place.

2 Run a row of thread-basting in the middle of the narrow second border and $1/2$ in (12 mm) in from the outer border edges.

3 Machine-quilt in the inner and outer black borders, avoiding the narrow striped border. As you quilt the inner borders, take the quilting into the edge triangles, removing the pins as you get to them. Keep the quilting fairly open to avoid distortion and leave approximately $1/2$ in (12 mm) on the edge of the outer border unquilted.

FINISHING

Note: Refer to the detailed instructions for "Binding", "Rod Pocket" and "Labeling your Quilt" on page 21.

1 Trim the excess batting and backing, leaving a $2^1/2$ in (6.5 cm) wide border. Thread-baste or pin-baste the raw edges together to stop any movement when attaching the bindings.

2 Measure the quilt vertically. Mark this measurement onto two of the $1^3/4$ in (4.5 cm) wide binding strips, using the chalk pencil. Halve and quarter both the strips and the sides of the quilt. Attach the bindings to the sides, using a $3/8$ in (1 cm) seam allowance. Turn the sewn bindings to the back and whipstitch them in place. Trim the excess length from the ends.

3 Repeat for the top and bottom borders, leaving an extra 1 in (2.5 cm) at both ends for turning the ends over the corners. Make sure the edges of the quilt are right in the fold so the bindings are full.

4 Attach a rod pocket to the back for hanging, and label your quilt.

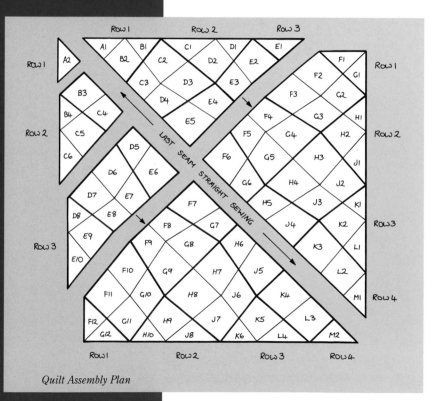

Quilt Assembly Plan

Fireworks

The design for this quilt is formed when four units with the same contrasting color combination are grouped together.

The units are made up of even and uneven logs. The two fabrics in the uneven logs alternate to form a spinning effect. I used fabrics that I normally wouldn't use together; use this quilt to extend your color confidence and use colors that you would not normally choose.

Finished size: 30 in (76 cm) square

FABRIC PLACEMENT

On a design wall, make a fabric mock-up of the colors you want to combine and stand back to see if they work. Do this for all thirteen main inner groups, making a fabric placement plan to follow. Take your time with this step. When you are satisfied, make a smaller version and paste it onto paper or leave the pieces on the wall and replace them with the pieced group. Don't be afraid to make changes as you go along.

DRAFTING

See the Quilt Layout Plan on page 65.
Note: Refer to the detailed instructions for "Drafting the Units" on pages 6–10.

Photocopy the layout plan. The units for this quilt are drafted in two sections: inner units and edge triangle units. The inner units are outlined with heavy lines on the Quilt Layout Plan. Draft the edge triangle units after the body of the quilt has been pieced.

For the inner units and logs:

Note: Even though there are repeated units in this quilt, I recommend that you draft everything.

1 On graph paper, draft all thirteen inner groups. Refer to the Quilt Layout Plan for the direction in which to draft the logs. The logs in each group are drafted

identically with three logs on either side of the center (Fig. 1). The even logs are all 3/8 in (1 cm) wide. The uneven logs must be no wider than 5/8 in (14 mm) at the wide end; the narrow end of the outside uneven log must be no narrower than 1/4 in (6 mm). If they are any narrower, you won't be able to trim the seam allowances from the outside stitching line. The inside narrow ends can be as narrow as you wish. The size of the units will determine the width of the uneven logs. The smaller the unit, the narrower the wide ends of the uneven logs will be. The logs spiral in a clockwise direction from the center.

When drafting a group, you can also mark the piecing order and the placement of the black and the black-and-white-striped fabrics. The top and bottom units in each group of four, have black on the longest (outside) even logs. The two side units in each group have a black-and-white-striped fabric on the longest (outside) even logs.

2 Cross each group off the photocopied layout plan as you draft it.

3 Turn the drafted groups over and transfer all the identification marks, piecing order and fabric placement to

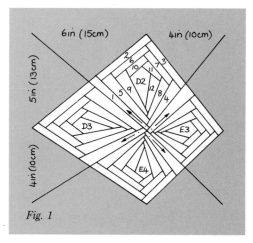

Fig. 1

YOU WILL NEED

Note: Fabric quantities are calculated for 44 in (112 cm) wide fabric. The specified amounts are generous.

- 24 in (60 cm) of black-and-white-striped fabric
- 32 in (80 cm) of black fabric for the unit piecing and the binding
- 20 in (50 cm) of white fabric
- 16 in (40 cm) of medium gray fabric
- 16 in (40 cm) of pale blue fabric
- 4 in (10 cm) each of twenty-six fabrics, sorted into thirteen pairs, for the inner units (You may repeat some of these fabrics if you wish.)
- 2 in (5 cm) each of sixteen fabrics for the edge triangle units, sorted into eight pairs
- 39 in (1 m) of fabric for the backing
- 39 in (1 m) of Pellon batting
- basic sewing and drafting equipment
- neutral-colored thread for unit piecing
- black thread for joining the rows and binding
- 2 1/2 yd (2.2 m) of medium-weight interfacing
- one skein of embroidery floss to match the backing fabric

this side. Mark a directional arrow at the top of each unit.

MARKING THE FOUNDATIONS

Note: Refer to the detailed instructions for "Preparing and Marking the Foundation" on pages 11–12.

1 From the interfacing, cut thirteen 6 in (15 cm) wide strips. Press the strips to pre-shrink them, then cut them into 6 in (15 cm) squares. You will need seventy-six foundations.

2 Mark the foundations for all the inner groups. Transfer all identification marks, piecing order, fabric placement and the directional arrow at the top of each unit.

CUTTING THE FABRIC

Note: Begin by cutting the following amounts; you can cut more as required.

1 From the black fabric and the black-and-white-striped fabric, cut four 1 1/4 in (3 cm) wide strips.

2 From each of the gray and blue fabrics, cut four 1 in (2.5 cm) wide strips.

3 From the white fabric, cut one 2 1/2 in (5.75 cm) wide strip.

4 From the pairs of fabrics, cut two 1 1/4 in (3 cm) wide strips from each. Work with one pair of fabrics at a time.

PIECING THE INNER UNITS

Note: Each unit of a group is pieced beginning with the same contrasting fabric in the first (shortest) uneven log. This forms the pattern when adjacent units are joined. For example, if the pair of fabrics are red and green and you start every unit with the green fabric, the red fabric will be the last uneven log sewn. This uneven log touches the adjacent unit. If you want the green to touch, then begin piecing with the red fabric (Fig. 2).

1 Roughly cut the unit centers from the white strip. To do this, lay the marked foundation over the white strip, centering it so there is a seam allowance extending beyond the marked lines of the center shape. Roughly cut the required length off the strip. Repeat for all the unit centers.

2 Piece the four units for one group.

3 Following the instructions for "Joining the Units into Groups" on page 15, join them to form the group. Leave the straightest seam to be the last joined. Most seams will have to be released, so sew from edge to edge, backstitching at the dots.

4 Place the completed group on the design wall, using the one remaining visible direction arrow to position it correctly.

5 Piece all the inner unit groups.

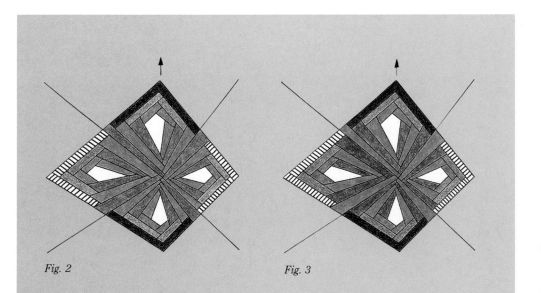

Fig. 2   *Fig. 3*

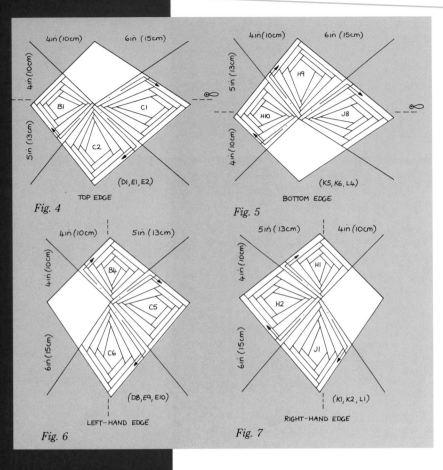

Fig. 4 — TOP EDGE
4in (10cm) 6in (15cm)
4in (10cm)
5in (13cm)
B1 C1
C2
(D1, E1, E2)

Fig. 5 — BOTTOM EDGE
4in (10cm) 6in (15cm)
5in (13cm)
4in (10cm)
H9
H10 J8
(K5, K6, L4)

Fig. 6 — LEFT-HAND EDGE
4in (10cm) 5in (13cm)
4in (10cm)
6in (15cm)
B4
C5
C6
(D8, E9, E10)

Fig. 7 — RIGHT-HAND EDGE
5in (13cm) 4in (10cm)
4in (10cm)
6in (15cm)
H1
H2
J1
(K1, K2, L1)

DRAFTING AND PIECING THE TRIANGLE UNITS

For the edge triangle unit groups:
Note: These groups are formed by piecing three complete units. Two of these units extend beyond the outside edges of the quilt. The excess is trimmed away after the quilt top has been assembled.

There are two edge triangle groups on each side of the quilt. Draft the four groups, following figures 4–7 and using the measurements given. Label them with the piecing order and fabric placement.

To maintain the pattern formed with the black-and-white-striped fabric, follow the directions carefully and study the fabric placement figures 8a–8d.

For the top and bottom edge triangle groups:

The two outside units in each set (the ones to be trimmed later) have black-and-white-striped fabric on the outside even logs. The single inside unit has black on the outside even logs.

For the side edge triangle groups:
The two outside units in each set have black on the outside even logs. The single inside unit has black-and-white-striped fabric on the outside even logs.

Mark two sets of foundations for each group. Each set will have different identification numbers. Make sure the repeat groups are labeled correctly.

Piecing the Triangle Groups

The units for these groups are pieced in exactly the same way as the inside units. Make a fabric mock up on the design wall to audition fabric placement around the sides. When you are satisfied, piece the units and join them into their groups of three. For the first two units, sew from the outside edge to outside edge. Press this seam open. Sew the next seam from the outside edge, but stop at the center dot and backstitch. Press the seam allowance toward the outside.

DRAFTING AND PIECING THE CORNER TRIANGLE UNITS

These are made up of two triangles per corner unit. As they repeat, only draft logs onto triangles A1 and A2. Follow the drafting direction shown in figure 9. Mark the piecing order. Turn the paper over and transfer the markings to this side.

Fabric Placement

Audition the fabrics for the corners as you did for the bulk of the quilt. To maintain the pattern formed by the striped fabric in the corners, follow the table below and color diagrams (Figs. 10 and 11) for fabric placement.

A1 and A2, M1 and M2
black-and-white-striped fabric on the longest outside even log (A1 and M2); black on the remaining outside even log (A2 and M1) (Fig. 10).

F1 and G1, F12 and G12
black on the longest outside even log (G1 and F12); black-and-white-striped fabric on the remaining outside even log (F1 and G12) (Fig. 11).

Referring to the table, mark one corner triangle unit at a time, labeling it with identification numbers, piecing order and the fabric placement.

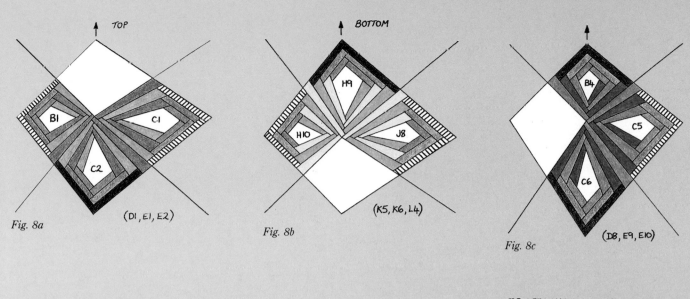

Fig. 8a

TOP

B1

C1

C2

(D1, E1, E2)

Fig. 8b

BOTTOM

H9

H10

J8

(K5, K6, L4)

Fig. 8c

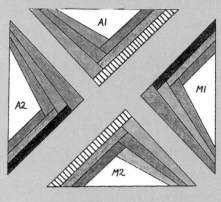

B4

C5

C6

(D8, E9, E10)

Fig. 8d

TOP

H1

H2

J1

(K1, K2, L1)

Fig. 9

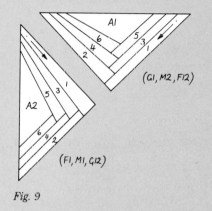

A1

6 5

4 3 1

2

A2

5 3 1

6 4 2

(F1, M1, G12)

(G1, M2, F12)

Fig 10

TOP LEFT-HAND CORNER

A1

A2

M1

M2

BOTTOM RIGHT-HAND CORNER

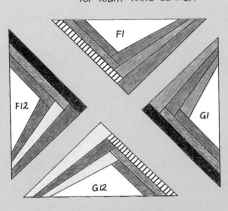

TOP RIGHT-HAND CORNER

F1

F12

G1

G12

BOTTOM LEFT-HAND CORNER

Fig. 11

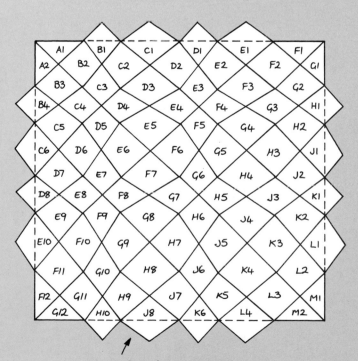

Excess trimmed away leaving
3/8 in (1cm) seam allowance.

Fig. 12

Marking the Foundations

Note: Refer to the detailed instructions for "Preparing and Marking the Foundation" on pages 11–12 and "Edge and Corner Triangle Units" on page 12.

Cut a 4 in (10 cm) wide strip of interfacing. Mark the foundations, making sure you mark each corner triangle with the appropriate identification number.

Piecing

Piece the triangles, one pair at a time. Stay-stitch and trim the excess down to 3/8 in (1 cm) on all three sides. Join the triangles together to form the corner unit, sewing edge to edge. Place the corner in position. Repeat for the other three corner units.

ASSEMBLY

Note: Refer to the Quilt Assembly Plan and the detailed instructions for "Joining Groups to Form Rows or Sections" on page 16.

1 The groups are joined together to form rows. Sew from edge to edge, but you must backstitch at the corner dots as some seam allowances must be released.

Detail of four joined units, showing the spinning effect.

2 Join rows 1, 2 and 3 together and rows 4 and 5 together to form two sections, then join the two sections. Press all the seams open.
3 Press the back of the quilt top first to make sure the seam allowances are flat, then press gently on the front.
4 Using the long ruler and rotary cutter, trim the excess units away from the outside edge triangle groups, leaving a 3/8 in (1 cm) seam allowance all around the edges (Fig. 12).

LAYERING

Note: Refer to the detailed instructions for "Layering" on page 20.
1 Assemble the three layers of the quilt.
2 Using long quilter's pins and beginning in the middle and working outward, pin each group making sure you catch all three layers.
3 Baste just inside the edges and again about 3/4 in (2 cm) in from the first row.

TYING

Note: Refer to the detailed instructions for "Tying" on pages 20–21.
1 Turn the quilt over. Starting at the center join, tie at all the major seam junctions. Don't go through to the front.
2 After tying, remove all the pins. Trim the edges of the backing and batting even with the quilt edges.

FINISHING

Note: Refer to the detailed instructions for "Binding", "Rod Pocket", and "Labeling Your Quilt" on page 21.
1 Cut four 1 3/4 in (4.5 cm) wide strips of binding fabric across the width of the fabric. Measure and attach, using a 3/8 in (1 cm) seam.
2 Bind the sides first. Turn the binding to the back of the quilt and hand-sew it down. Repeat for the top and bottom edges, remembering to leave an extra 1 in (2.5 cm) at both ends for turning under to cover the corners.
4 Attach a rod pocket for hanging and attach a label on the back.

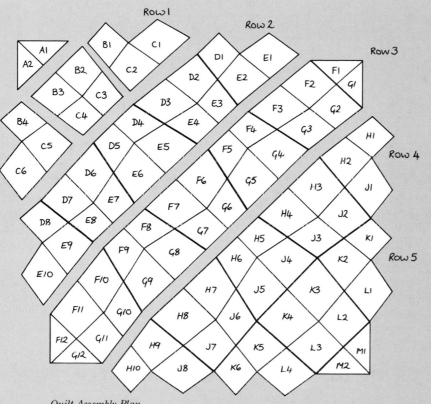

Quilt Assembly Plan

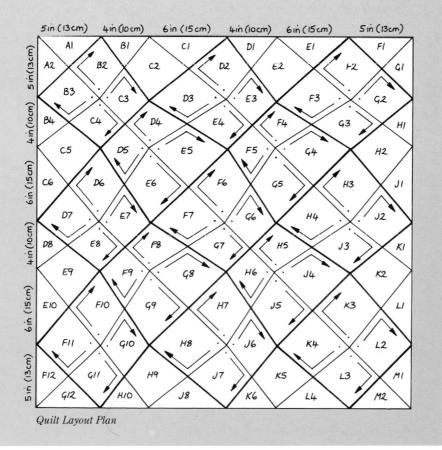

Quilt Layout Plan

Just a Little Bit

YOU WILL NEED

Note: Fabric amounts are calculated for 44 in (112 cm) wide fabric. The quantities given are generous. Unless otherwise stated (and except for the backing fabric), all fabrics are solids.

- **8 in (20 cm) of four or five different burgundy-colored to rust-colored fabrics**
- **8 in (20 cm) of four or five different medium dark to medium green fabrics**
- **4 in (10 cm) of four or five beige fabrics**

Continued on page 68

Several different patterns appear in this quilt; there is a yellow grid and, if you look closely, you will notice green and red Ohio Stars appearing to float across the surface of the quilt. These were not anticipated – they just happened.

Finished size: 45 in (114 cm) square

DRAFTING THE GROUPS

See the Quilt Layout Plan on page 69.
Note: This quilt has groups of units which repeat (inner groups S and T; edge triangle groups U, V, W and X; corner triangle group Y). Refer to the detailed instructions for "Drafting the Units" on pages 6–10 and the group drafting diagrams (Figs 1–7) below.

Follow the given measurements in the diagrams for each group, draft all seven of them. Do not draft the logs at this stage. Label each sheet of graph paper with the name of the quilt, the group letter and the unit identification numbers, for example, "Just a Little Bit, Group S, Units A3, A4, B1 and B2". Mark the log drafting arrow in the appropriate position in each unit.

Drafting the logs onto the inner groups S and T:

1 Following the direction arrows, draft $5/16$ in (8 mm) wide logs onto all inner units. The number of logs in the units vary: all A units (A1, A2, A3 and A4) have five logs on either side of the center; all B units (B1, B2, B3 and B4) have four logs on two sides and three on the other two sides. Begin by drafting three logs on all four sides, beginning at the dot and working in the direction of the arrow (Fig. 8). Still going in the same direction, draft two more logs (numbers 13 and 14) (Fig. 9).

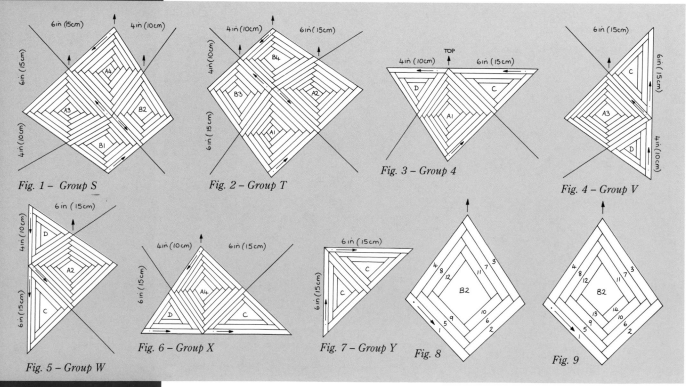

Fig. 1 – Group S

Fig. 2 – Group T

Fig. 3 – Group 4

Fig. 4 – Group V

Fig. 5 – Group W

Fig. 6 – Group X

Fig. 7 – Group Y

Fig. 8

Fig. 9

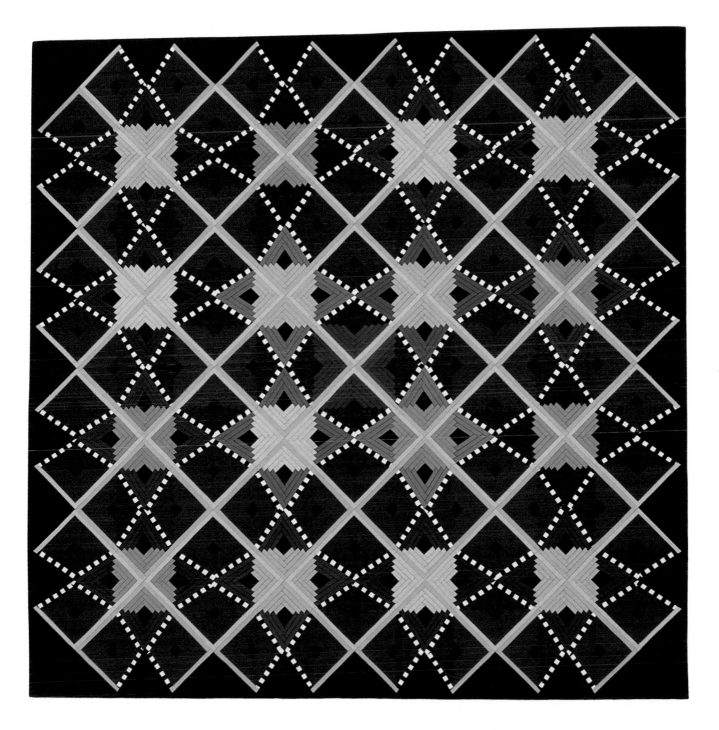

- 8 in (20 cm) of four or five different red fabrics
- 8 in (20 cm) of bright gold/orange fabric
- 8 in (20 cm) of bright yellow fabric
- 8 in (20 cm) of black-and-white-striped fabric
- 8 in (20 cm) of royal blue fabric for the unit centers
- 50 in (125 cm) of navy fabric for the piecing and binding. Cut the four binding strips 1¾ in (4.5 cm) wide first on the lengthwise grain and use the remainder for the piecing
- 3 yd (2.5 m) of fabric for the backing
- 50 in (130 cm) of 48 in (122 cm) wide Pellon batting
- basic sewing and drafting supplies
- 4¾ yd (4.2 m) of medium-weight interfacing
- two skeins of embroidery floss to match the backing fabric
- navy thread to match the binding fabric
- neutral-colored thread for piecing

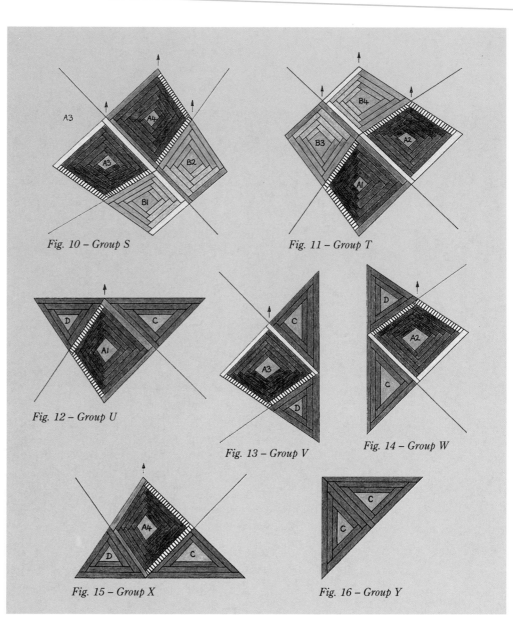

Fig. 10 – Group S

Fig. 11 – Group T

Fig. 12 – Group U

Fig. 13 – Group V

Fig. 14 – Group W

Fig. 15 – Group X

Fig. 16 – Group Y

Drafting the logs onto the edge and corner triangle groups:

Note: Groups U, V, W and X all consist of one inner unit and two edge triangles C and D. Each group is repeated four times. Both edge triangles have two logs on either side of the center with three logs on the long outside edge.

Follow the detailed instructions on pages 6–10 and draft the logs onto the A units as before, then draft ⅜ in (1 cm) wide logs onto each of triangles C and D.

Group Y consists of two C triangles. Draft the logs onto them in the same way as before.

FABRIC PLACEMENT

Refer to the color placement diagrams (Figs 10-16) above and mark the color placements onto the outside logs. The centers of all the units are royal blue.

When all the units are drafted and the colors are indicated, turn the drafted groups over and transfer all the identification numbers and color placements to this side. Mark a direction arrow at the top of all units.

MARKING THE FOUNDATIONS

Note: Refer to the detailed instructions for "Preparing and Marking the Foundation" on pages 11–12.

For the inner Groups S and T:

1 Cut twenty-two 6 in (15 cm) wide strips of interfacing. Cut them into 128 squares, 6 in (15 cm).

2 Mark the units. You can mark them all or mark only enough for several inner groups at a time. Transfer all the identification marks. Pin the four units for each group together after marking.

For the edge triangle Groups U, V, W and X:

1 Cut three 6 in (15 cm) wide strips of interfacing. Cut them into sixteen 6 in (15 cm) squares.

2 Mark each inner unit (A1, A2, A3 and A4) four times – a total of sixteen units. Transfer all the markings.

3 Cut four 4 in (10 cm) wide strips of interfacing. Mark sixteen C and sixteen D triangles.

PIECING

For the inner groups:

1 From the fabrics, cut the following (cutting more as required):
  ■ four 1 in (2.5 cm) wide strips from the bright yellow, orange and black-and-white-striped fabrics;
  ■ four 1¹/₂ in (4 cm) wide strips from the royal blue fabric for the unit centers; and
  ■ one 1 in (2.5 cm) wide strip each from one of the assorted reds, burgundy, beige and green fabrics.

2 Referring to figures 10 and 11, begin to piece the units, working with one group at a time. Make sure you trim the excess seam allowances down to 3/8 in (1 cm) after stay-stitching.

3 Following figure 17, join the units to form pairs, then join two pairs to form the group. Press all the seams open. This is a straight seam. Sew from the outside edge to the outside edge. Both inner groups S and T are joined the same way.

4 Select another group of red, burgundy, beige and green fabrics and repeat the process for another group. Piece all the inner Groups S and T (sixteen of each).

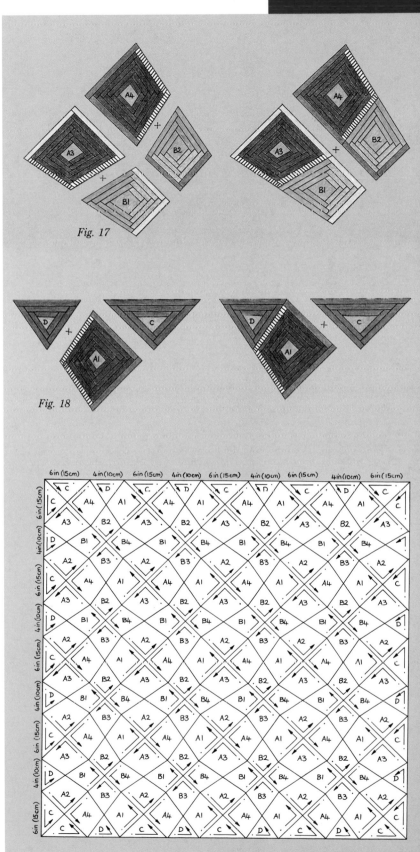

Fig. 17

Fig. 18

Quilt Layout Plan

Pin them on the design wall after joining, with the one remaining visible direction arrow indicating the top of the group.

For the edge triangle Groups U, V, W and X:

1 Cut four 1¼ in (3 cm) wide strips from the navy fabric. Cut more as required.

2 Working with one group at a time and referring to figures 12–15, piece the inner unit and triangles. Join them together, following figure 18. Sew all the seams from edge to edge and press them open. Pin them in place on the design wall. Repeat for the other groups.

For the corner triangle Group Y:

These groups each consist of two C triangles. Mark four foundations and piece them as before. Join them into pairs. Press the seams open and pin them in place on the design wall.

JOINING THE GROUPS INTO ROWS

1 Referring to the Quilt Assembly Plan and the detailed instructions on page 16, join the groups into diagonal rows with the triangle groups joined to the top left- and bottom right-hand corners. All seams are straight, sewn from edge to edge and pressed open. Pin-match all seams and along marked sewing lines.

2 Join the rows together to form two sections, then join the sections together to form the quilt top.

LAYERING

Note: Refer to the detailed instructions for "Layering" on page 20.

1 Join the backing fabric (and the batting, if necessary).

2 Assemble the three layers and pin-baste. Thread-baste around the edges of the quilt and again about 1½ in (4 cm) in from the edges.

TYING

Note: Refer to the detailed instructions for "Tying" on pages 20–21.

Turn the quilt over and tie on the back at all major seam junctions or at each group. Remove the basting pins from the front.

FINISHING

Note: Refer to the detailed instructions for "Binding", "Rod Pocket", and "Labeling Your Quilt" on page 21.

This quilt does not have borders, so the binding is attached directly to the edge triangle units using a ³⁄₈ in (1 cm) seam allowance.

1 Using the pre-cut navy binding, measure and cut the bindings. Leave an extra 1 in (2.5 cm) extending on both ends of the top and bottom bindings for turning under at the corners.

2 Sew the bindings to the sides first, then to the top and bottom.

3 Add a rod pocket for hanging, if you wish. Don't forget to sew a label on the back.

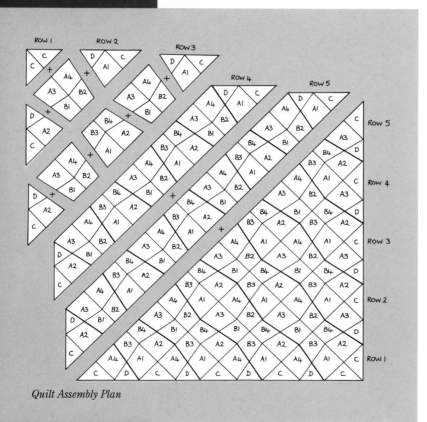

Quilt Assembly Plan

Adrift

YOU WILL NEED
**Note: Fabric amounts
are calculated for 44 in
(112 cm) wide fabric.
The specified amounts
are generous. It is hard
to give precise yardage
/metrage for this quilt.
I used leftover fabrics for
the piecing and found
myself running out of
some and having to
introduce others. So
begin with plenty of
choices. Multicolored
prints work well, as
they give a wide range
of variations when cut
into strips.**

- **8 in (20 cm) of fifteen
  to twenty dark,
  medium/ dark and
  bright fabrics – the
  more you have, the
  more interesting the
  units will be**

Continued on page 74

This is a wonderful quilt to make. It uses a wide variety of dark, bright and light prints. Use leftover strips of fabric from other projects or use it as an excuse to buy more! Fat quarters or fat eighths are ideal. I incorporated a mixture of cottons and lightweight furnishing fabrics in this quilt to get a big enough range of light fabrics. Try to keep fabric weights about the same.

This quilt is one of the most difficult in the book. Follow all the diagrams carefully and reread the detailed instructions on pages 6–10. When joining the rows and sections, just take it slowly and pin frequently.

Finished size: Approximately 37 in x 46 in (94 cm x 117 cm)

PREPARATION FOR DRAFTING
See the Quilt Layout Plan on page 74. A combination of wide and narrow log widths is used in all of the inner units. The edge triangle units all have wide logs.

There are three types of unit variations within the quilt (Figs 1–3):

Variation 1 (Fig. 1)
This unit has narrow logs on two sides of the center and wide logs on the other two sides. The drafting begins with two narrow logs, then two wide logs, but always finishes with two narrow logs in the center. In some cases, this results in a very small center shape. The wide logs are $^1/_2$ in (12 mm), the narrow logs are $^5/_{16}$ in (8 mm).

The number of logs drafted around the center will vary, depending on the size of the unit. Some will have four narrow and three wide logs; others will have five narrow and four wide logs. When drafting, make sure you begin and end with narrow logs. The larger the unit, the more logs.

Variation 2 (Fig. 2)
These units are identified on the layout plan with an 'f' under the unit identifying number. These are drafted with the first round of logs $^1/_2$ in (12 mm) wide; the next round of four logs are narrow at $^5/_{16}$ in (8 mm) wide. All the remaining logs in the unit are wide. As you draft this unit you will find that sometimes there will be an even number of logs on either side of the center and sometimes not. It depends on the size of the unit.

Variation 3 (Fig. 3)
These are the edge and corner triangle units. They have all wide logs at $^1/_2$ in (12 mm). Most triangles will have two logs on two sides of the center and one on the outside edge. The smaller triangles, for example F1, will have two logs on one side only. Otherwise,

Variation 1
B2, C2–C4, D2, D3, D5, D6, E2–E5, E7, E8, F2–F6, F9, F10, G2-G9, G11, G12, H2, H3, H5–H10, H13, H14, J3, J4, J6–J12, J14, J15, K3, K4, K6–K11, K14, K15, L3, L4, L7–L12, L14, L15, M3, M4, M6–M13, N3, N4, N7, N8, N10, N11, O3, O4, O6–O9, P3, P4, P6, P7, R3, R4, R5, S3

Variation 2
B3, C5, D4, E6, E9, F4, F7, F8, F11, G10, G13, H4, H11, H12, H15, J2, J5, J6, J13, J16, K2, K5, K12, K16, L2, L5, L6, L13, M2, M5, N2, N5, N6, N9, O2, O5, P2, P5, R2, S2

Variation 3
A1, A2, B1, B4, C1, C6, D1, D8, E1, E10, F1, F12, G1, G14, H1, H16, J1, J17, K1, K17, L1, L16, M1, M14, N1, N12, O1, O10, P1, P8, R1, R6, S1, S4, T1, T2

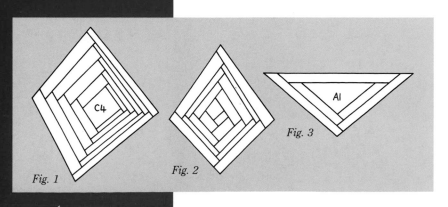

Fig. 1

Fig. 2

Fig. 3

- 10 in (25 cm) of at least twelve to fourteen light fabrics, including whites, creams, white-on-white, pale blues, yellows and pinks

Note: The backs of some fabrics can also be used if your selection is limited. The total amount required is approximately 3¹/₂ yd (3.5 m).

- 50 in (128 cm) of fabric for the backing
- 50 in (128 cm) of 48 in (122 cm) wide Pellon batting
- 10 in (25 cm) of fabric for the binding, cutting across the grain (you will have to join strips to get the required length) or 50 in (128 cm), cutting on the lengthwise grain
- 5 yd (4.7 m) of interfacing
- two skeins of embroidery floss for tying
- basic sewing and drafting supplies

Quilt Layout Plan

DRAFTING THE UNITS AND LOGS

Note: Refer to the detailed instructions for "Drafting the Units" on pages 6–10.

1 Draft the units onto graph paper. Work with one group of units at a time, beginning with the group B2, B3 + C3 and C4. Place the identifying number in the middle and the log drafting direction arrow in each unit (Fig. 4).

2 Study the Quilt Layout Plan and the unit variation table on page 72 for the log widths. Begin at the dot and work in the direction of the arrow. Turn the graph paper over and transfer all the dots and identification marks to this side. Also, mark a direction arrow at the top of each unit. This is very important.

3 The next group of four units to be drafted is C2, C3/D3 and D4. You already have the unit C3 drafted so just put a cross in it. Work group by group, moving across one increment of the grid at a time as you draft the units. Then work downward.

Note: Some units are repeated and are marked as reversals. As this can be confusing, I found it easier to draft out all the units, rather than fiddle with reversals. I have supplied some of the easiest repeat units. They are the variation 2 units running down both sides of the quilt. The units on the right-hand side of the quilt need to be reversed because of the direction in which the logs are drafted. To mark a reversal, mark the foundation on the right side of the graph paper – the side you drafted the units and the logs onto. Make sure you label it with its correct number. If you marked B3 as a reversal, name it J2 and so on. (B3 – J2, C5 = K2, D7 = L2, F9 = M2, F11 = N2, G13 = O2, H15 = P2, J16 = R2, K16 = S2.)

MARKING THE FOUNDATIONS

Note: Refer to the detailed instructions for "Preparing and Marking the Foundations" on pages 11–12.

For the inner groups:

1 From the interfacing, cut twenty-four 6 in (15 cm) wide strips. Cut them into 142 squares, 6 in (15 cm).
2 Mark the foundations for the inner units as instructed. For the reversals, mark the foundations on the right side of the graph paper. Transfer all identification marks and directional arrows.

For the edge triangle groups:

1 Cut five 4 in (10 cm) wide strips from the interfacing.
2 Mark the triangles. The edge triangles repeat. Make sure you mark each triangle with its appropriate identification number and the * in the outside edge seam allowance, so you know where to place it.

A1
Mark it sixteen times. The repeats are A2, C1, C6, F1, F12, H1, J1, K17, L1, L16, N 12, O1, R6, T1 and T2.

B1
Mark it eight times. The repeats are D8, G1, G14, M1, M14, P1, S4.

D1
Mark it twelve times. The repeats are B4, E1, K1, E10, N1, H16, J17, R1, S1, O10 and P8.

CUTTING THE FABRIC

Note: All the narrow logs are pieced using the dark, medium and bright fabrics. The

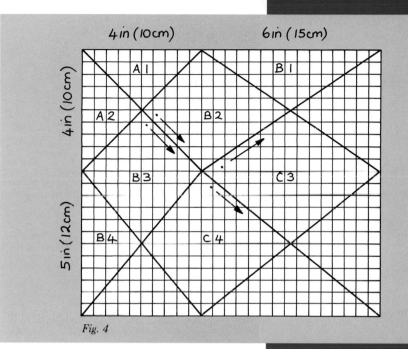

Fig. 4

wide logs are pieced using the light fabrics. The unit centers are all light.

1 Cut one 1 1/4 in (3 cm) wide strip from all the light fabrics.
2 Cut one 1 in (2.5 cm) wide strip from all the dark, medium and bright fabrics. Cut more fabric strips as you need them.

PIECING

Refer to the detailed instructions for "Foundation Piecing" on page 13 and begin to piece the units. Try to have a different fabric in the outside logs where units meet, so you don't have two fabrics the same, side by side.

Some of the units taper to a point. When this occurs, leave plenty of fabric extending at the top or bottom of the strip. If you don't, the strip will not cover the intended area. Pin the strip on the sewing line and fold it open to check that you have left enough allowance extending at the ends.

1 Piece all the inner units for the quilt, pinning them up on the design wall as you go. Use the direction arrow to position the units correctly. Make sure you have trimmed each unit, leaving an exact 3/8 in (1 cm) seam allowance.
2 Piece all the triangle units and pin them in position.

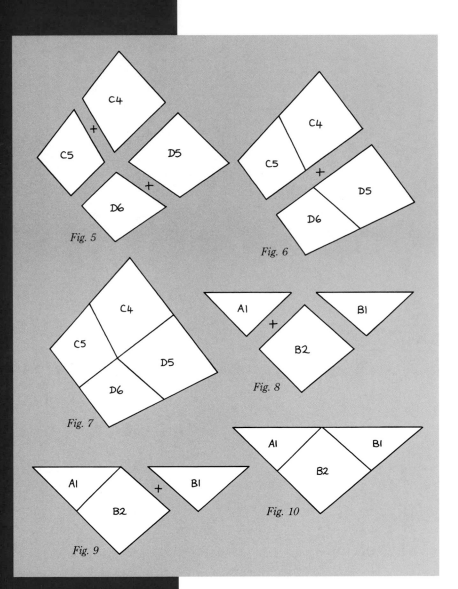

Fig. 5

Fig. 6

Fig. 7

Fig. 8

Fig. 9

Fig. 10

to start at the outside edge, go one stitch past the first dot, backstitch and sew to the end dot, backstitch and sew to the end. Release the beginning and ending stitches to free the seam allowances, when necessary.

3 Join the rows together to form the sections. Where seam allowances have to be released, sew from corner dot to corner dot within a group, keeping the released seam allowances out of the way.

4 Construct all four sections, then join sections A and B, then C and D. Join the two resulting sections together to form the quilt top.

LAYERING

Note: Refer to the detailed instructions for "Layering" on page 20.

1 Press the quilt top well, checking to make sure the seams are all open. There should be a 3/8 in (1 cm) seam allowance, extending beyond all the outside units. The binding is attached with a 3/8 in (1 cm) seam directly to the sides of the quilt.

2 Assemble the layers. Pin-baste frequently, beginning in the center and working outward. Run a row of thread-basting around the outside edge and again 1 in (2.5 cm) inside the stay-stitching.

TYING

Note: Refer to the detailed instructions for "Tying" on pages 20–21.

Tie the back of the quilt at the major seam junctions, starting with the center group. Space the ties out, so the layers are held firmly and evenly.

FINISHING

Note: Refer to the detailed instructions for "Binding", "Rod Pocket", and "Labeling Your Quilt" on page 21.

1 Trim the excess batting and backing even with the edges of the top.

2 For binding cut on the crosswise grain, cut three 1 3/4 in (4.5 cm) wide strips. Cut one in half and join one half to each of the other two strips with a diagonal

ASSEMBLY

The quilt is assembled in four sections labeled A, B, C and D on the Quilt Assembly Plan. Refer to the detailed instructions for "Joining Units into Groups" on pages 15–16.

1 Follow figures 5-10 and the Quilt Assembly Plan for the unit groupings. These are outlined with thick black lines on the assembly plan. Pin-match frequently and press all the seams open. Join the inner groups and edge triangle groups in each section, then place each group on the wall in its correct position.

2 Join the inner groups and edge triangle groups into rows, in each section. When sewing the groups together, remember

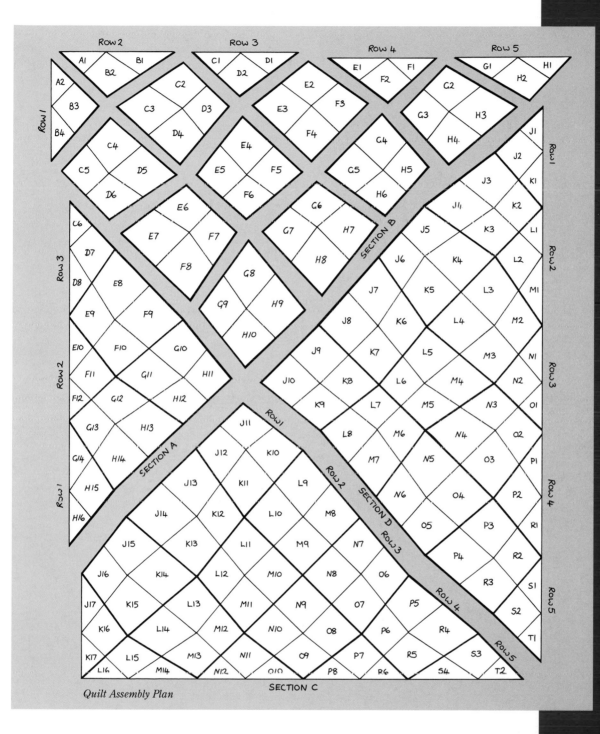

Quilt Assembly Plan

seam. This is the binding for the sides.
    Cut two 1³/4 in (4.5 cm) wide
strips plus an extra 2 in (5 cm) for
turning around the corners. This is the
binding for the top and bottom.

3 For binding cut on the lengthwise grain,
    cut two strips, 50 in (127 cm) long and
    1³/4 in (4.5 cm) wide. This is the binding
    for the sides.

Cut two strips 42 in (107 cm) long
and 1³/4 in (4.5 cm) wide. This is the
binding for the top and bottom.

4 Using a ³/8 in (1 cm) seam, sew the long
    binding strips to the quilt sides first. Turn
    them to the back and hand-sew in place.
    Repeat for the top and bottom bindings.

5 Attach a rod pocket for hanging and sew
    a label on the back.

Troubleshooting

Most of the problems that can occur while making the quilts in this book are solved simply by practicing the techniques. The more you do, the better you'll become.

Some of the more common problems are as follows:

■ Seam allowance bulk keeps pushing the machine foot to one side, resulting in stitching being off the marked line. This can be solved in two ways:

1 Trim the seam allowance to about ⅛ in (3 mm) from the stitching line. To do this, it is sometimes better to press the seam open first, then trim it.

2 Trim the seam allowance so that it is just inside the area to be covered but leaving the next marked sewing line clear. However, this does make the finished units bulkier and would make it harder to machine-quilt.

If the problem persists, experiment with using different machine feet.

■ Pleating is where one end of the sewn strip is not finger-pressed quite enough, resulting in a strip that is wider or narrower at one end. That is, the strip has not been rolled open correctly. Quite often it is not noticed until the whole unit has been pieced. To avoid pleating, roll the strip and finger-press first, then press with the iron and, finally, trim the seam allowance.

■ Having trouble remembering the color-piecing sequence can be avoided if you mark the color run onto the foundation. If this is just outside the outer marked line, it won't be seen. If a unit has a particular color order, cut snippets of the fabrics and tape them down on the photocopied layout plan. Label it and refer back to it, when you are piecing.

Alternatively, if the quilt is constructed using repeat blocks, first construct one of each of them, then you will have something to refer back to when making the remainder of the blocks.

■ Making small cuts in the foundation when trimming the seam allowances can be a problem. Small nicks are not really a problem, however, if you make a large cut, place a piece of removable tape over the cut, then sew the next strip in place. Remember to remove the tape before pressing.

■ You didn't realize that a group of units were to be treated as a set-in seam. When joining units, begin stitching at the outside edge. When you get to the first corner dot, sew a couple of stitches, backstitch as far as the dot, sew to the end dot, backstitch here, then sew to the edge. If the seam is to be set in, you only have to undo the few stitches at the beginning and the end of the row.

■ The unit is puckering and won't lie flat. This can be the result of many things: the interfacing used for the foundation is too light; the stitch length is too small, if so, lengthen it slightly; or you are pulling on the foundation as you sew, if so, let the machine do the pulling while you just guide it.

■ If you have to remove any stitching, do it from the fabric side rather than from the interfacing side. If you remove stitching from the interfacing side, you run the risk of accidentally tearing the interfacing with the seam ripper. If you need to remove stitching from two sewn units, break every third or fourth stitch and just pull the units apart.

■ If you are sewing a light fabric strip over a dark one, and the dark one shows through when the light strip is pressed, trim the darker seam allowance so it is fully hidden under the lighter one.

TIPS

■ Whenever I begin a project I always have a clear photocopy of the layout plan at hand. This enables me to mark off units as I mark the foundations. I also mark the units I have pieced with a fluorescent marker, so I can see at a glance those I have pieced.

■ Unless I am positive that I have all reversals and repeats correctly noted, I draft out every unit. There is nothing more frustrating than to piece a unit that doesn't fit anywhere.

■ If certain units are repeated in both drafting and color placement, make up one of each and use these as guides for the remainder.

■ Make fabric mock-ups. You only need small pieces of fabric. Pin them to the marked units as placement guides.

■ When marking units I always mark at least eight to ten at a time, then I place them on my design wall, with the marked side to the wall, in their correct position. This is very important, especially if the design has a particular color running from unit to unit. Always place the finished unit up on the wall after piecing.

■ If you don't have a design wall, use a curtain or, even better, a flannel sheet. Make a small pocket along one short edge that is big enough to fit a rod. Place a couple of picture or cup hooks in a wall and hang the sheet up. After finishing work for the day, simply take it down and gently fold it up. All the units will be in place the next time you hang it up.

■ When working with strips of fabric in color runs and gradations, I try to keep them in order by hanging them on a coat hanger. This way you can easily locate the strips you need, instead of having a tangled mess.

■ Don't fold the finished quilts, as they will develop a definite crease on the fold lines. I lay those that are not hung flat on a spare bed. Try to avoid strong light falling on the quilts, as this will fade them and cause the fabric to deteriorate.

■ There are many other books that deal with machine-quilting techniques. For this reason, I have not described them in detail.

Dedication

To my grandmother, who always told me to have faith in myself and always finish what I started. She also told me that you won't know what you are capable of until you try.

Acknowledgments

I would like to thank Judy Poulos and Karen Fail who asked me to write this book and believed that I had the skill and dedication to do so. Thanks also to my family, who I'm sure felt neglected during the last two years but seldom complained, and gave me support and encouragement, and to my children, who are my strongest critics.

Thank you Margaret Miller for unknowingly planting a seed that grew into a strong tree covered in quilts.